PRAISE FOR THE SYMBIS+ ASSESSMENT
AND *STRENGTHEN YOUR MARRIAGE*

When it comes to helping couples, Les and Leslie Parrott are at the top of my list. We've literally taken thousands of engaged couples through the SYMBIS Assessment and we use SYMBIS+ with all the married couples we can. That's why this guidebook is so valuable. It helps couples apply insights from the SYMBIS+ Report directly into their relationship.

Steve Blair,
Church of the Highlands, Birmingham, Alabama

I love this guide. We use the SYMBIS+ Assessment with married couples at our church and it's been incredibly effective. This guidebook takes it to a new level—making the SYMBIS+ Report even more personalized and powerful. The assessment and resource are like twin engines propelling you to a stronger and healthier marriage.

Matthew Drew,
Elevation Church, Charlotte, North Carolina

The Parrotts have done it again! Just when we thought that the SYMBIS+ Assessment system that we use exclusively in our counseling center couldn't possibly get better, it just did! Now we have another great resource to use with our couples that will augment the SYMBIS+ Report and help them do the work it takes to have a healthy and blessed marriage. Tools like these from Les and Leslie make our job and mission so much easier. This is a must-have resource in your counseling and marriage ministry toolbox. Don't miss out!

Rich Villafaña,
The House Counseling Center Pastor, Modesto, California

Strengthen Your Marriage is like rocket fuel for the already powerful SYMBIS+ Assessment. These two tools—the assessment and the guidebook—are an incredible combination. You are going to love what this does for your relationship.

Kevin Cordner,
Christian Life Center, Dayton, Ohio

STRENGTHEN YOUR
MARRIAGE

RESOURCES BY LES AND LESLIE PARROTT

BOOKS

51 Creative Ideas for Marriage Mentors
Becoming Soul Mates
The Complete Guide to Marriage Mentoring
Dot.com Dating
Getting Ready for the Wedding
The Good Fight
Healthy Me, Healthy Us
Helping Couples
The Hour That Matters Most
I Love You More (and workbooks)
L.O.V.E.
Love Is . . .
Love Talk (and workbooks)
Love Talk Devotional
Making Happy
The Marriage Mentor Training
Manual (for Husbands/Wives)
Meditations on Proverbs for Couples
The Parent You Want to Be
Questions Couples Ask
Real Relationships (and workbook)
Saving Your Marriage Before It
Starts (and workbooks)
Saving Your Marriage Before It Starts Devotional
Saving Your Second Marriage Before
It Starts (and workbooks)
Trading Places
Your Time-Starved Marriage

VIDEO CURRICULUM

I Love You More

Love Talk
Saving Your Marriage Before It Starts
Saving Your Second Marriage Before It Starts

AUDIO PAGES®

Love Talk
Relationships
Saving Your Marriage Before It Starts
Saving Your Second Marriage Before It Starts

BOOKS BY LES PARROTT

7 Secrets of a Healthy Dating Relationship
3 Seconds
25 Ways to Win with People
(coauthored with John Maxwell)
The Control Freak
Crazy Good Sex
Helping Your Struggling Teenager
High-Maintenance Relationships
The Life You Want Your Kids to Live
Love Like That
Love the Life You Live (coauthored
with Neil Clark Warren)
Once Upon a Family
Shoulda, Coulda, Woulda
You're Stronger Than You Think

BOOKS BY LESLIE PARROTT

The First Drop of Rain
God Made You Nose to Toes (children's book)
Soul Friends
You Matter More Than You Think

GAIN THE EXPERIENCE OF OVER 5 MILLION COUPLES

STRENGTHEN YOUR
MARRIAGE

Personal Insights into Your Relationship

A Companion to the

SYMBIS+
ASSESSMENT

Drs. Les & Leslie Parrott

#1 *New York Times* Bestselling Authors

ZONDERVAN
BOOKS

ZONDERVAN BOOKS

Strengthen Your Marriage
Copyright © 2021 by Les and Leslie Parrott

Requests for information should be addressed to:
Zondervan, *3900 Sparks Dr. SE, Grand Rapids, Michigan 49546*

Zondervan titles may be purchased in bulk for educational, business, fundraising, or sales promotional use. For information, please email SpecialMarkets@Zondervan.com.

Library of Congress Cataloging-in-Publication Data

Names: Parrott, Les, author. | Parrott, Leslie L., 1964- author.
Title: Strengthen your marriage : personal insights into your relationship / Les Parrott, Leslie Parrott.
Description: Grand Rapids : Zondervan, 2021. | Includes bibliographical references. | Summary: "Perfect for any couple, and an ideal companion to the renowned SYMBIS Assessment, this guidebook walks couples through an even deeper experience of their unique relationship. Chock-full of practical insights, real-life action steps, no-guilt exercises, and fun discussion starters, this guidebook will bring couples closer than ever"— Provided by publisher.
Identifiers: LCCN 2020043071 (print) | LCCN 2020043072 (ebook) | ISBN 9780310361640 (trade paperback) | ISBN 9780310361657 (ebook)
Subjects: LCSH: Marriage. | Marriage—Religious aspects—Christianity. | Married people—Psychology.
Classification: LCC HQ734 .P2225 2021 (print) | LCC HQ734 (ebook) | DDC 306.81—dc23
LC record available at https://lccn.loc.gov/2020043071
LC ebook record available at https://lccn.loc.gov/2020043072

Published in association with Yates & Yates, www.yates2.com.

Cover design: Curt Diepenhorst
Cover photo: Hybrid Images | Getty Images
Interior design: Denise Froehlich

Printed in the United States of America

21 22 23 24 25 /LSC/ 10 9 8 7 6 5 4 3 2 1

To Colonel Blair.
We salute your heartfelt dedication to strengthening marriages.
Your vision and passion for helping couples on a large scale is an inspiration,
and we're proud to be partners in your exceptional efforts.

We dedicate this book to you, Steve,
and to your entire Dream Team of marriage champions.

CONTENTS

GETTING THE MOST FROM YOUR SYMBIS+ GUIDEBOOK

Action is the foundational key to all success.

—PABLO PICASSO

We know at least one important thing about you: You're taking action. You're being pro-active in your relationship. You two are building the best marriage possible—whether you are moving from bad to better or good to great. How do we know? Because you're reading these words, we know you've already taken the SYMBIS+ Assessment (or you're about to). And this guidebook is dedicated to helping you maximize this powerful experience.

We also know you are working with one of our trained and certified SYMBIS Facilitators—a counselor, a coach, or a member of the clergy (you can find one near you at SYMBIS.com). They have a passion for helping you. And your SYMBIS Facilitator will be your expert guide in unpacking your customized SYMBIS+ Report.

Before jumping in, we want to answer some questions you may be asking.

WHY THE NAME, SYMBIS?

As a psychologist (Les) and a marriage and family therapist (Leslie), we wrote our first book years ago: *Saving Your Marriage Before It Starts*. SYMBIS for short. Little did we know that nearly two million couples would read it and the accompanying his/her work-books. We never imagined that it would catch the attention of national media like *Oprah*, *Good Morning America*, CNN, Fox, and all the rest. But it did. We were soon speaking in cities across the country and sometimes around the world. SYMBIS was a hit.

HOW DID THE ASSESSMENT COME ABOUT?

As the popularity of the book *Saving Your Marriage Before It Starts* grew, we wanted to do everything we could to ensure it was making a difference. After all, we are both social scientists, and we put a premium on trusted research. So, with a team of fellow researchers at our university, we discovered that newlywed couples could benefit tremendously when linked to a more experienced couple who would invest in their success. We called them Marriage Mentors. And we trained dozens of them on our local campus. That program grew beyond our university, and we eventually launched our online Marriage Mentoring Academy (see MarriageMentoring.com) where we have now trained more than a quarter million seasoned couples to come alongside less experienced couples.

But that's not all. We wanted to help singles find a good match, so we worked with Dr. Neal Warren to found the first online service, backed by scientific studies, dedicated to helping people find the optimal chemistry with another person. We called it eHarmony. And millions of people have found the love of their life because of it. And if there is one thing we learned in that process, it is that technology can be leveraged to nearly magical levels to provide insights and tools for healthy relationships.

So the idea of creating an online assessment for couples, particularly on the front end of their relationship as they were preparing for marriage, was a natural. We launched the SYMBIS Assessment years ago and quickly discovered something we didn't anticipate: our SYMBIS Facilitators were beginning to use this pre-marriage assessment not only with engaged and newlywed couples, but with couples at all stages. That's when we realized it needed to be adapted and customized for couples at any age or stage. And it needed to eliminate anything related to engagement and add information that experienced couples need. We called it *Strengthen Your Marriage (Because It's Sacred)* or SYMBIS+.

WHY SHOULD WE TAKE THE ASSESSMENT?

It's one thing to read a marriage book or attend a marriage seminar. They can add tremendous value to your relationship. But the SYMBIS+ Assessment Report you are about to explore is going to take your personal insight and action plan to a new level. Why? Because it is designed specifically for the two of you. It is highly customized. The information on your report does not pertain to any other couple.

For example, one of the sections of the report will help you understand how your personalities work together. It will show you how to best leverage your shared chemistry. And the paragraphs it provides are personalized. In fact, nearly forty thousand variables go into each paragraph. That means that nobody else in the world will have the same paragraph describing their personality as you do. We are pulling levers behind the proverbial scenes to bring you the most accurate and helpful information we can. That's the magic of the SYMBIS+ Report. As we often say, it puts the cookies on the bottom shelf so you can easily understand and receive the information that's going to make a difference.

DOES THE ASSESSMENT "GRADE" OUR RELATIONSHIP?

No. It's not something you can pass or fail. You don't receive a "score." Think of it as a customized road map for lifelong love—a map that is specific to your relationship. It's upbeat and positive. And most importantly, because you are working with a trained Facilitator who is an expert in unpacking your report, it is actionable. It provides you with practical steps. You won't be left wondering, "Now what?" You'll know how to set your sails for the direction you both want to go.

WHAT SHOULD WE KNOW ABOUT TAKING THE ASSESSMENT?

If you haven't already done so, it's easy. You simply connect with one of our trained and certified SYMBIS Facilitators (use the Facilitator Finder at SYMBIS.com) and they'll set you up to answer a series of items online. You'll do so separately, and it will take each of you about twenty-five minutes or so. Once you complete the questionnaire, your Facilitator receives a copy of your report and will begin debriefing your report with you.

WHAT SHOULD WE KNOW ABOUT OUR OWN REPORT?

It's typically comprised of seventeen pages, but if you have a blended family or some other aspects to your relationship, it could be a page or two more. And each page of your report is different. Each page is devoted to a specific topic, such as "expectations" or "communication."

More than likely, your Facilitator will explore a couple of pages of the report with you in each session (typically an hour). However, you might be doing this in a small group, a class, or maybe even a retreat. And if so, that experience can vary. Regardless, your Facilitator will likely reveal only the pages you'll be exploring in that particular session. Why? Because it's more conducive to a positive learning experience. But don't worry, your Facilitator will likely provide you with your entire SYMBIS+ Report as you conclude your debriefing sessions together.

HOW SHOULD WE USE THIS GUIDEBOOK?

The purpose of this resource is to augment your experience with your Facilitator. Each page of your SYMBIS+ Report has a corresponding chapter in this guidebook. Most often, you will explore a specific chapter after having debriefed the corresponding page of your report in a session with your Facilitator. Or, once you complete all of your debriefing sessions with your Facilitator, you may want to use the guidebook as a way of taking that experience to an even deeper level. In fact, you can have some fun and incorporate it into some date nights together. Each chapter includes a few conversation starters that are ideal for that. Regardless, there's really no right or wrong way to use it. And, of course, your Facilitator will certainly offer some input on how you can best use this resource too.

DO WE EACH NEED OUR OWN COPY OF THE GUIDEBOOK?

Ideally, each of you should have your own copy of the guidebook. As you'll soon see, there are exercises that have you record information in this guidebook that you will each want to do separately (in fact, seeing each other's information before you record your own ruins the results). So, yes, we recommend that you each have your own guidebook. We've worked closely with our publisher to have these produced in an economical way for that very reason.

Well, there you have it. We've done our best to anticipate your preliminary questions. But if we didn't answer a question you have, let us know. You can contact us at help@ SYMBIS.com. And, of course, you can also ask your SYMBIS Facilitator.

We wish you the very best as you explore your customized road map for lifelong love.

DRS. LES & LESLIE PARROTT
LESANDLESLIE.COM
SEATTLE, WASHINGTON

Chapter 1

MARRIAGE MOMENTUM

Momentum solves 80 percent of your problems.

—John C. Maxwell

They call it the Shinkansen. We call it the bullet train—and millions of passengers use it on a daily basis to crisscross Japan. So when we had the opportunity to visit Tokyo recently, we couldn't pass up a chance to travel at over 150 mph on rails.

"Look at these comfy seats," Leslie said as we slipped into our row.

"They have footrests," I chimed in. "And free Wi-Fi."

"Yes, and this button over here will commence your seat warmers," an impeccably uniformed train attendant remarked. He overheard us talking in our American accents as he came by with a small food cart containing bento boxes.

"Your English is fantastic," I said to him with a smile.

"Oh, I studied in America for four years." He went on to point out other amenities on the train and continued: "Did you notice that we were on time, to the second? Punctuality is a priority. And we have a spotless safety record."

The proud attendant wanted to be sure we Americans were rightfully impressed by his country's modern marvel. And we were. But most impressive of all was the engineering of this amazingly smooth and fast ride. The train uses two sets of magnets, one that pushes the train up off the track and another that propels it forward. That's what provides the momentum. And it does so with next to no friction. Ingenious.

If you've ever been near a conventional train when it starts to move, you see (and hear) the engine wheels work hard to turn and pull the rest of the cars. It creaks and screams under the strain. Eventually the attached cars slowly begin to roll. But once they begin rolling, the engines relax. Momentum takes over, so much so that the train (typically traveling at 40 mph) has difficulty stopping. It needs at least a mile once the brakes are applied to get it even close to a stop. That's the power of momentum.

> Successful people keep moving. They make mistakes, but they don't quit.
> —Conrad Hilton

Once momentum is achieved, friction is the name of the game. More friction means more work to maintain the hard-earned momentum. Without friction, velocity increases and momentum comes almost effortlessly.

The same is true in marriage. When a couple is contending with friction of any kind—financial stress, parenting challenges, physical health issues, communication meltdowns, and so on—momentum requires more work. Friction slows us down. We have to dig in and really exert effort. But once we overcome frictional forces, our momentum helps us move forward and even break through obstacles with ease.

WHAT IS MARRIAGE MOMENTUM?

Just like a locomotive engine that pulls train cars forward, the two of you are the twin engines of your marriage. And the more friction challenging your relationship right now, the harder you'll need to work to move forward. Of course, you'll never be friction-free. Nobody has discovered marriage magnets that lift you above troubles and propel you forward without effort. Even couples who have high momentum aren't trouble-free. But their momentum makes those troubles easier to overcome.

WHAT IS YOUR CURRENT LEVEL OF MARRIAGE MOMENTUM?

On page 2, in the upper left corner of your SYMBIS+ Report, you'll find a dial with a red needle, much like a speedometer. It's an indicator of everything on your report. In other words, when we look at all of the answers you provided through the questionnaire and compare them with common standards, we can give you a sense of how much momentum you currently have toward enjoying a fulfilling marriage.

Not only does the red needle move across the dial, but the report also notes whether your momentum is high, medium, or low.

If you could instantly change one thing about your circumstances or about you (not your spouse) to improve your marriage momentum, what would it be and why?

The Benefits of Increased Momentum

Regardless of whether you are *high*, *medium*, or *low* on your momentum, every couple benefits from gaining more momentum that leads to a stronger and healthier relationship.

MOMENTUM INCREASES ENERGY

Nothing is more demotivating and energy sapping than working on something, only to find out it does not matter. When you're working hard but that hard work has no payoff, energy is depleted. But once you see your efforts making a positive difference, energy increases. The SYMBIS+ Assessment, along with your SYMBIS Facilitator, will ensure that your efforts are channeled into areas that have a proven payoff. So if your momentum is low, along with your energy level, you'll soon see that improving.

Rate your current energy level as you begin the SYMBIS+ experience . . .

NEXT TO NONE   RARING TO GO

1	2	3	4	5	6	7	8	9	10

Explain: _____

_____

_____

MOMENTUM OVERCOMES OBSTACLES

When your momentum is low, you can become your own worst enemy. You tend to blame your circumstances—or each other—because you feel stuck and immobilized by struggles. But when momentum improves, people no longer blame circumstances; they look for the circumstances they want and, to paraphrase George Bernard Shaw, if they can't find them, they make them. In other words, they proactively look for solutions. Couples with high momentum don't see obstacles as insurmountable; they take action to overcome them.

Rate your desire to look for solutions rather than blame circumstances . . .

WHATEVER									EXCITED
1	2	3	4	5	6	7	8	9	10

Explain: _____

_____

_____

MOMENTUM INSPIRES DREAMS

Success breeds success. When an athlete is on a roll, playing extremely well, they elevate their performance. Even in a game of pickup basketball, players will try to get the ball to the player who is "hot." Why? Because they are "in the zone" and more likely to make the shot. They have momentum. And because of it they set their sights higher. They suddenly believe they have a chance at the championship. Consider athletes such as tennis star Serena Williams, basketball great Michael Jordan, or quarterback Tom Brady. The stronger your momentum, the bigger your dreams. So if your marriage momentum is high, consider where you are headed together. Give care and thought to your dreams together.

We share specific and inspiring dreams together as a couple . . .

NOT REALLY   FOR SURE

1	2	3	4	5	6	7	8	9	10

Explain: _____

_____

_____

CAN WE IMPROVE MARRIAGE MOMENTUM?

Absolutely. Let's say you are currently contending with incredible friction and your momentum is low. Maybe it feels like you can't even get the wheels on your proverbial marriage engine to roll forward. That's okay. If you are committed to your relationship, you can make it happen. Commitment keeps the spark plugs firing. You may need to lean heavy into your commitment when it feels like that's all you have, but it will come through. You'll find the leverage you need to get moving in the right direction. The pages of your SYMBIS+ Report are going to help you do just that.

Now, what if your momentum is high? You are moving along at a smooth and steady clip with very little friction in your lives. Count your blessings. And don't take this season for granted. Why? Because eventually, somewhere down the tracks, you will meet up with something you weren't expecting. It happens to even the healthiest of couples. It could be infertility, a career shift, an accident, or even infidelity. Marriage momentum isn't fixed, and it doesn't guarantee that you won't encounter problems. You will. Life can change in an instant. So, if you are currently enjoying high momentum, this is prime time to fine-tune your marriage engine. And every page of your SYMBIS+ Report will show you exactly how to do that. Even more, it will take your momentum from good to great. After all, even the happiest of couples can always improve. This experience for you is not merely preventive intervention. You'll see immediate benefits on numerous fronts as you gain even more momentum.

> Never surrender to the momentum of mediocrity.
> —Marlon Brando

On a scale of 1 to 10 how would rate your commitment to work on improving your overall marriage momentum? What would improve your level of commitment?

A FINAL THOUGHT

Scientists calculate momentum by multiplying the mass of the object (like a train) by the velocity of the object. It is an indication of how hard it would be to stop the object. We think your marriage momentum works by a similar formula:

Marriage Momentum = (2 x Commitment) x Direction

Your **marriage momentum** equals the level of **commitment** each of you brings to the relationship, multiplied by the **direction** you want to go. If you are both committed to improvement (even if only in small increments), and you agree on the destination of a strong marriage together, you will become unstoppable as a couple. Your marriage is sure to go the distance. You can count on lifelong love every bit as much as you can count on the Shinkansen being on time in Tokyo.

Chapter 2

MARRIAGE MINDSET

---

*The mind has a powerful way of attracting things
that are in harmony with it, good and bad.*

—Idowu Koyenikan

Harold courted her for three years, walking her to the theater on warm nights and bringing flowers and chocolates to her uncle's store where she was the cashier. But sixty-five years after she said "I do," Harold is still trying to woo Marion—even as Alzheimer's disease has erased most of her memory. It shut down her command of the family piano and her ability to make the brisket Harold loved so much. The disease robbed her of even remembering her husband most of the time. But while she doesn't recognize him, Harold says, he still recognizes Marion.

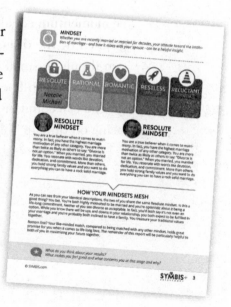

That's why every week Harold visits Marion at the center where she receives round-the-clock care from professionals. He comes into her room with decorations, party hats, a little birthday sign with her name on it, and two cupcakes from her favorite bakery.

Harold asks Marion: "Do you know what day it is?"

"No," Marion says. "What day is it?"

"It's your birthday and we're going to celebrate," Harold tells her with a big grin.

7

A couple of Marion's nurses know the weekly drill and join Harold as they sing "Happy Birthday" and then applaud as Marion blows out the candle on her buttercream cupcake.

"Oh, my, this is the best cupcake I've ever had," is Marion's typical response.

"I thought you'd like it, sweetie," Harold tells her.

He gives her a sweet kiss on the forehead, tells her she's beautiful, and hands her a little gift to open—sometimes a piece of jewelry he gave her years earlier and sometimes a familiar photo of the two of them. Whatever it is, Marion is opening it for the first time and delights in the celebration.

> There is no such thing in anyone's life as an unimportant day.
> Alexander Woollcott

So does Harold. After they eat their cupcakes, Harold holds her hand for a few minutes and reminisces for a bit or listens to music they both enjoy. But mostly he celebrates Marion and the life they shared for more than six decades. "I still picture her as the cashier and I can't believe how blessed I was to be her husband. We had a great life together."

When asked why he celebrates her birthday every week, Harold says, "Marion always loved to celebrate birthdays. So why not make every visit I have with her a special celebration?"

Why not, indeed? Harold has a marriage mindset that wouldn't allow for anything but the best for his bride.

 First, what thoughts do you have after reading about how Harold celebrated his wife even after she began suffering from Alzheimer's disease? Second, what insight did you gain for yourself in completing this exercise?

Celebrating Each Other

As we jump into the topic of your marriage mindsets, let's heed the unspoken advice of Harold and do a quick exploration of how well the two of you are doing when it comes to respecting, honoring, and celebrating each other.

When was the last time you felt fortunate to be with your partner—then told them?
A. Past twenty-four hours   B. Past week   C. Past month   D. Not sure

Does your partner feel noticed, admired, and valued by you?
A. For sure   B. Probably   C. Hopefully   D. *Cringe*

How frequently do you carry out a thoughtful act that shows your partner you were thinking specifically of them—expecting nothing in return?
A. Every day   B. Every week   C. Every month   D. Not sure

Does your spouse feel good about your sex life (frequency and quality)?
A. I know so   B. I think so   C. I hope so   D. I'm not sure

What's the ratio of positive comments to negative comments you make to your spouse in a typical week?
A. Way more + than –   B. More + than –   C. More – than +   D. Way more – than +

Would your partner say they feel celebrated by you?
A. For sure   B. Probably   C. Hopefully   D. Not sure

Tally the number of each letter:
A ____   B ____   C ____   D ____

The more your answers fall toward the A and B side, the better you feel you're doing at celebrating your spouse. Of course, this exercise is only as reliable as your honesty in taking it. So how about checking in with your partner to see how they feel about it.

UNDERSTANDING THE FIVE MINDSETS

You've already explored your two marriage mindsets, noted on this page of your SYMBIS+ Report with your SYMBIS Facilitator. What we want to do here is give you a more detailed description, based on the research, of each one of them. No need to read about the ones that don't pertain to you unless you'd like to do so. Here's a brief summary of each:

THE RESOLUTE MINDSET

DEFINITION

Res-o-lute /'reze,loot/
Adjective: Admirably purposeful, determined and unwavering.

- This segment, 22 percent of the population, prizes marriage and holds tight to an unyielding determination to make it go the distance. When it comes to marriage, they are dedicated to ensuring that it's for life.
- More than most, Resolutes have carefully considered what they want for their life and one thing is certain: they want to be married. More than likely, they resolved this important milestone for themselves some time ago. In fact, it's such a significant part of their life plan that they may not have even considered the option of not being married.
- Resolutes are true believers when it comes to matrimony. They are more than twice as likely as others to say that divorce is not an option for them. They resonate with words like *devotion*, *dedication*, and *commitment*.
- More than other people, they are also likely to want to have children at some point. In fact, only 2 percent of Resolutes say they never want children. They plan to invest in their family, making it a supreme priority in their life. And it will most likely be the greatest source of their life's happiness.

It is our attitude at the beginning of a difficult task which,
more than anything else, will affect its successful outcome.
—William James

THE RATIONAL MINDSET

DEFINITION

Ra-tion-al /'raSH ənl /

Adjective: Agreeable to logic, sound judgment or good sense.

- This segment, 23 percent of the population, takes a more practical approach to marriage than most. They view this lifelong commitment with more caution than others.
- Rationals guard their heart. They're doing what they can to protect it from harm. That's why, relative to others, they tip the scales a bit more toward rationality than romance when it comes to matrimony.
- They don't buy into the mystical idea of finding their *soulmate*. They view finding a potential partner to marry as a more rational endeavor that will inevitably require serious work.
- When asked what they expect from marriage, Rationals, more than other segments, expect the road to lifelong matrimony to have its share of bumps. They expect marriage to be personally fulfilling, for sure, but they know that fulfillment comes with a price. And that price is hard work.
- Rationals know that marriage requires effort and sacrifice. They know it requires compromise, learning the art of give and take. They're not expecting to be "lucky in love." In fact, they tend to agree with Thomas Jefferson when he said, "I'm a great believer in luck, and I find the harder I work the more I have of it."

THE ROMANTIC MINDSET

DEFINITION

Ro-man-tic /rō'mantik /

Adjective: Inspired by the ideal of affection and love.

- This segment, 19 percent of the population, brings a heavy dose of *idealism* to marriage. Romantics expect love to be lived out with unending passion and ongoing intimacy.
- Love, for the Romantic, is a bit like a movie. It is adventurous, poetic, starry-eyed, chivalrous. In a word, love for the Romantic is idyllic.

- They see love as standing strong, overcoming all, and being the source of unending bliss.
- Romantics believe in a soul mate. In fact, they are nearly twice as likely as the average person their age to say, "There's only one perfect marriage partner for me." So they bring a great deal of idealistic hope and not a short supply of unconscious pressure to their marriage.

THE RESTLESS MINDSET

DEFINITION

Rest-less /restləs /
Adjective: Characterized by discontent or uneasiness.

- This segment, 22 percent of the population, is typically pretty slow to enter marriage. They generally take their time to get to it
- You've heard the phrase, "ants in your pants," right? It usually refers to a fidgety kid who never seems to sit still. This same restlessness, however, is found in this segment, especially when they are young adults.
- The idea of "settling down" is not an easy pill to swallow for this mindset. They're not looking for more responsibility.
- Words like *dependable, conscientious, loyal, serious,* and *responsible* seldom enter the picture. Their "go for it" attitude is focused on fun. And the fewer responsibilities they take on the more fun they believe they'll have.
- Restless Mindsets typically needs to work on the skills that make marriage work (communication, conflict management, empathy, and so on).

THE RELUCTANT MINDSET

DEFINITION

Re-luc-tant / riəlɔktənt /
Adjective: Exhibiting resistance or unwillingness.

- This segment, 14 percent of the population is "not the marrying kind." More than any other segment, Reluctants are cynical about matrimony. In fact, it's the only segment to lack a desire to wed, probably because their own homes were examples of how *not* to do it.

- Not only is their marriage motivation very low, but one in five say they never want children.
- When studying the differences between the "marrying kind" and the "non-marrying kind," Reluctants not only are more accepting of divorce but are more likely to question the very value of marriage.
- What Reluctants expect from marriage can be summed up in two words: *not much*. If anything, they mistakenly expect to lose their identity in exchange for very few payoffs.

 As you review the various marriage mindsets, how well do you feel your category sums up some of your attitude toward marriage? Why?

Did you know that marriage researchers actually talk about married couples "sculpting" each other? In scientific studies of marriage, it's literally called the *Michelangelo effect*. In subtle ways, we are reinforcing patterns in each other via countless little interactions, positive or negative moments. That sculpting you do—regardless of your marriage mindset—can either reveal more of who your partner is or it can hold your partner captive by limiting their potential.

Just as scientists have found that our brains recognize and categorize our moments—as either as positive, negative, or neutral—they've also studied the impact of positive-to-negative interaction ratios in our relationships. They have found that this ratio can be used to predict—with remarkable accuracy—whether or not we succeed in marriage.

It all began with noted psychologist John Gottman's exploration of positive-to-negative ratios in marital interactions. Happy relationships, he found, are characterized by a ratio of 5:1. This means that for every negative statement or behavior such as criticizing or nagging, there are five positive statements—Gottman calls it the *magic ratio*. He and his colleagues predicted whether seven hundred newlywed couples would stay together or divorce by scoring their positive and negative interactions in one fifteen-minute conversation between each husband and wife. Ten years later, the follow-up revealed that they had predicted divorce with 94 percent accuracy.

Incredible, isn't it? A positive mindset can change everything for a couple. Positivity that prompts celebrating little moments with your spouse by simply saying, "I love you," "I'm so glad I'm married to you," "I'm proud of you," and so on, not only increases a couple's happiness but also evokes the best in each other, helping both partners come closer to reaching their best selves. This kind of positivity chips away at whatever is holding us captive. When we recognize, honor, and celebrate each other, we're freed up to be the best person and partner we can be. It's up to us to sculpt the best marriage our love can afford.

 How are you doing when it comes to the "magic ratio" of positive-to-negative interactions in your marriage? How would you like to improve it? Be specific.

And in the end, it's not the years in your life that count. It's the life in your years.
—Abraham Lincoln

Chapter 3

WELLBEING

---

*The curious paradox is that when I accept myself
just as I am, then I can change.*

—CARL R. ROGERS

Did you know you were born smiling? Modern 4D ultrasound technology shows that developing babies appear to smile even in the womb. After they're born, babies continue to smile (initially mostly in their sleep) and even blind babies smile in response to the sound of the human voice.

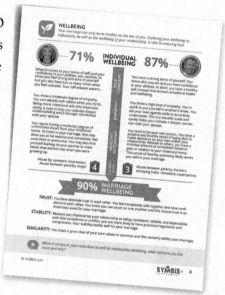

A thirty-year longitudinal study at UC Berkeley examined the smiles of students in an old yearbook and measured their wellbeing and success throughout their lives.[1] By measuring the smiles in the photographs, the researchers were able to predict how fulfilling and long lasting their marriages would be, how highly they would score on standardized tests of wellbeing and general happiness, and how inspiring they would be to others. The widest smilers consistently ranked highest in all of the above.

When it comes to understanding your current state of wellbeing, we can do better than having you study how much each of you were smiling in your baby pictures or your high school yearbook. This page of your SYMBIS+ Report provides a snapshot of the various components that are most predictive of emotional wellbeing: self-concept, empathy, and autonomy. We'll unpack each of these in this chapter as well as the elements that go into the wellbeing of your marriage relationship: trust, stability, and similarity.

Before we jump in, let's be clear about what we mean by the term *wellbeing*. For our purposes, it has to do with emotional, psychological, and spiritual health. If you are coping well with your environment and living a fulfilled and fruitful life, your wellbeing is at a high level. You are enjoying the presence of positive emotions such as contentment and joy and finding meaning and purpose in a life well lived.[2]

YOUR INDIVIDUAL WELLBEING

As the top of this report page says, your marriage can only be as healthy as the two of you. So we begin by exploring your individual perspectives before exploring your relationship's wellbeing.

UNDERSTANDING PERCENTILE NUMBERS

We'll say it straightaway. Your percentile numbers are not "scores." So don't think of them as a grade or a ranking. Think of them more as a current temperature reading. And like the temperature in your home, you can adjust it by making some changes. In other words, these numbers are not permanent. They change. They fluctuate depending on decisions you make and attitudes or perceptions you conjure. In all likelihood, you won't have the same percentile number for wellbeing a year from now, or maybe even a month from now. Your number is about your current *state*, not your ongoing *trait*.

With this understanding of your number, how do you feel about it? Do you think it's reasonable for it to be at this current level? Can you think of a particular issue in your life right now that is impacting it? If so, what is it and why is it shaping your wellbeing?

SELF-CONCEPT

Call it self-confidence, self-esteem, self-worth, self-perception, or self-regard. Whatever you call it, a person with a healthy self-concept has an attitude of flexibility, preserves harmony and dignity under stress, is honest about accomplishments as well as short-comings, and is comfortable giving and receiving compliments. Such people are secure and comfortable in their own skin. The closer our real self is to our ideal self, the stronger our self-concept.

True You

In the shapes below write a few words for each self—who you feel you are (real self) in comparison to who you'd like to be (ideal self). This is not an exhaustive list, just three to five words in each area:

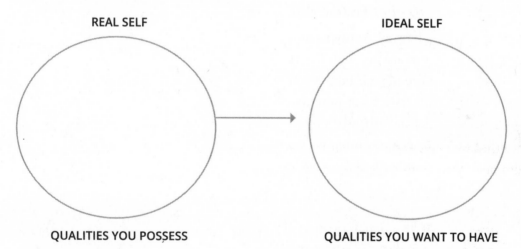

REAL SELF   IDEAL SELF

QUALITIES YOU POSSESS   QUALITIES YOU WANT TO HAVE

Now, on the line between them, indicate on a scale of 1 to 10 how far apart you feel your real self is from your ideal self (with 1 being extremely far apart and 10 being almost identical). Explain to your spouse why you feel this way and what you are doing, if anything, to move closer to your ideal self.

...ATHY

Your ability to put yourselves in each other's shoes as a couple is one of the most important skills you will ever develop. It soothes anger and engenders grace. It cultivates deeper understanding and intimacy. Empathy, especially when it is mutual, is at the heart of a loving marriage. Most of us think we empathize more than we actually do. After all, it's an intentional act. It doesn't happen without effort (unlike its close cousin, sympathy). Empathy requires both your head and your heart. You have to analyze as well as sympathize. Importantly, it's a skill that all of us can continually develop and improve.

> Love is not just looking at each other, it's looking in the same direction.
>
> —Antoine de Saint-Exupéry

Spouse's Shoes

Take a couple of minutes right now to imagine what it would be like to live in your spouse's shoes. What emotions would be new? What pressures or fears might you have? How would you feel differently about your career, about money, about your body, etc.? Ask your spouse questions if it helps you see the world more accurately from their perspective (don't make assumptions that could be wrong).

What did you learn from doing this exercise?

_____

_____

_____

What will enable you to empathize with your spouse more frequently?

_____

_____

_____

AUTONOMY

You might hear psychologists refer to autonomy as *individuation*. It's the process healthy people go through to achieve a sense of individuality that is separate from what others (typically parents, but others as well) think they should be.[3] It's a natural lifelong process, but sometimes we get stuck or stunted in developing an independent sense of self (because of unconscious guilt, shame, pain, or any number of reasons). Without autonomy, a person feels uncomfortable pursuing goals that diverge from the wishes of their family, for example. This can lead to overdependence on others, poor decision making, and a lack of personal meaning or purpose. In extreme cases, depression or anxiety can be the result.

Our Comfort Zone

What defeating message do you tend to play in your head that might be keeping you from fully achieving a sense of individuality? Give it some thought and be honest:

_____

_____

_____

Oftentimes, though we desire to achieve healthy autonomy, we fear stepping outside our proverbial comfort zone. In the outer ring of this diagram note anything that you've considered doing but haven't done because of fear or anxiety:

COMFORT
ZONE

Discuss what is keeping you from stepping beyond the boundary of your comfort zone. If you're feeling brave, allow your spouse to speak into this subject as well (but only if you are ready and willing).

CAUTION FLAGS

If you've ever watched a NASCAR race, you've seen officials wave a solid yellow flag so drivers know to slow down due to a hazard on the track. It could be debris, light rain, or an accident. This short section on this page of your SYMBIS+ Report is virtually the same thing. It's a "caution flag" to indicate that there are issues on your marriage track. They need to be tended to for the sake of your individual and relational wellbeing.

More than twenty-five potential cautions could show up here on your report, and typically they come in clusters. In other words, if a person has one caution flag, it's likely they have others as well. So don't be alarmed if several caution flags are indicated. The important thing is that you are aware of them and doing something proactive about them. That may include getting individual therapy (e.g., for depression), attending a sobriety group (e.g., for alcoholism), and so forth. Chances are you've already explored these issues with your SYMBIS Facilitator.

 What do you need to be doing, in very practical terms, to get help dealing with the caution flags that appear on this page?

YOUR MARRIAGE WELLBEING

The bottom portion of this page of your report not only reveals how your two personal positions on wellbeing combine but also factors in three additional elements that are important to your marriage. That's why your percentile indicator here is probably not the average or your two individual percentiles.

TRUST

In many ways, trust—a belief in your spouse's reliability—is the bedrock of your relationship. Every relationship falters when trust is questioned. A marriage is built on a pledge that requires confidence, conviction, and faith. Without trust, skepticism and doubt seep into the crevices of your relationship and instill uncertainty.

You've probably heard of, or maybe even participated in, a team-building exercise in which individuals deliberately allow themselves to fall, trusting that others in the group will catch them. Thankfully, the two of you don't need to experience a so-called trust fall in order to measure this important quality.

Truth and Trust

These questions can help you both gain more clarity on the trust in your relationship. Be sure to explain your answer and then talk through your reasoning. Also, it's important that both of you be ready for this little exercise. Don't do this if you are hungry, stressed or tired.

YES	NO	
		I'm happy to let my spouse know my passwords.
		I'm comfortable with my spouse randomly going through my phone.
		I have complete confidence that my spouse will follow through on a favor.
		I would blindly do what my spouse asks without explanation.
		I completely trust my spouse with a secret.
		I clarify before jumping to wild conclusion regarding my spouse.

Review your answers together when you are both rested, and be sure to have an open and non-defensive spirit as you process this information.

STABILITY

Instability creates anxiety. Whether it's around finances, careers, or health, instability heightens our fears and frustrations. Wild fluctuations can even send us into a panic. Why? Because human beings function best with stability. We like things smooth and steady, especially in marriage.

Where I Stand

Place an X along the continuums to indicate where you perceive yourself to be in relationship to your spouse.

AGREEABLE	DISAGREEABLE
CONSCIENTIOUS	CARELESS
WARM	COLD
RELIABLE	UNDEPENDABLE
EMOTIONALLY STABLE	EMOTIONALLY UNSTABLE
CALMING	ANNOYED
FLEXIBLE	INFLEXIBLE

Compare your answers with each other and discuss why you answered the way you did. Use specific examples when you can.

SIMILARITY

Whether articulated or not, everyone has a list of core values—beliefs or ideals deemed most desirable to them. For example, some prize open-mindedness over dependability while others might be exactly the opposite. Research reveals that the more values two people have in common, the easier and stronger their relationship.

Core Values

To delve deeper into your most important values, take a moment on your own to review this list of common personal values. Circle your top ten. As you do, you may find that some of these naturally combine. For instance, you might circle compassion, generosity, and service. You can sum that up by saying the common core value is "service to others." The point is just to use this list to help you become more articulate about what you value most.

ACCOUNTABILITY	CONTRIBUTION	EXCELLENCE	HUMILITY
ACCURACY	CONTROL	EXCITEMENT	INDEPENDENCE
ACHIEVEMENT	COOPERATION	EXPERTISE	INGENUITY
ADVENTUROUSNESS	CORRECTNESS	EXPLORATION	INNER HARMONY
ALTRUISM	COURTESY	EXPRESSIVENESS	INQUISITIVENESS
AMBITION	CREATIVITY	FAIRNESS	INSIGHTFULNESS
ASSERTIVENESS	CURIOSITY	FAITH	INTELLECTUAL STATUS
BALANCE	DECISIVENESS	FAMILY	INTELLIGENCE
BEING THE BEST	DEPENDABILITY	FIDELITY	INTUITION
BELONGING	DETERMINATION	FITNESS	JOY
BOLDNESS	DEVOUTNESS	FOCUS	JUSTICE
CALMNESS	DILIGENCE	FREEDOM	LEADERSHIP
CAREFULNESS	DISCIPLINE	FUN	LEGACY
CHALLENGE	DISCRETION	GENEROSITY	LOVE
CHEERFULNESS	DIVERSITY	GOODNESS	LOYALTY
CLEAR-MINDEDNESS	DYNAMISM	GRACE	MAKING A DIFFERENCE
COMMITMENT	ECONOMY	GROWTH	MASTERY
COMMUNITY	EFFECTIVENESS	HAPPINESS	MERIT
COMPASSION	EFFICIENCY	HARD WORK	OBEDIENCE
COMPETITIVENESS	ELEGANCE	HEALTH	OPENNESS
CONSISTENCY	EMPATHY	HELPING SOCIETY	ORDER
CONTENTMENT	ENJOYMENT	HOLINESS	ORIGINALITY
CONTINUOUS	ENTHUSIASM	HONESTY	PATRIOTISM
IMPROVEMENT	EQUALITY	HONOR	PEACEFULNESS

PERFECTION	RIGOR	SPEED	THOUGHTFULNESS
PIETY	SECURITY	SPONTANEITY	TIMELINESS
POSITIVITY	SELF-ACTUALIZATION	STABILITY	TOLERANCE
PRACTICALITY	SELF-CONTROL	STRATEGY MINDED	TRADITIONALISM
PREPAREDNESS	SELFLESSNESS	STRENGTH	TRUSTWORTHINESS
PROFESSIONALISM	SELF-RELIANCE	STRUCTURE	TRUTH-SEEKING
PRUDENCE	SENSITIVITY	SUCCESS	UNDERSTANDING
QUALITY	SERENITY	SUPPORT	UNIQUENESS
RELIABILITY	SERVICE	TEAMWORK	UNITY
RESOURCEFULNESS	SHREWDNESS	TEMPERANCE	USEFULNESS
RESTRAINT	SIMPLICITY	THANKFULNESS	VISION
RESULTS ORIENTATION	SOUNDNESS	THOROUGHNESS	VITALITY

Once you have your ten or so core values identified, compare your list with your spouse's list. Discuss how they match (or don't) and how you can appreciate and affirm each other's values when they are not overlapping.

Chapter 4

SOCIAL LIFE

---

*There is no substitute for the comfort supplied by
the utterly taken-for-granted relationship.*

—Iris Murdoch

You'd think that after all the time we humans have
had on this earth, we'd have made negotiating our
relationships a little simpler. It's not that we haven't
tried. But even our folk wisdom on relationships
raises more questions than it answers. Do birds
of a feather flock together, or do opposites really
attract? Does absence make the heart grow fonder,
or is out of sight out of mind?

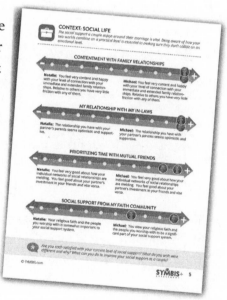

No doubt about it, in spite of all our good
intentions and sincere efforts, relationships are
rarely simple. A good indication of the complexity
of modern relationships, according to comedian
Jerry Seinfeld, is that greeting card companies
are forced to put out cards that are blank on the
inside: "Nothing—no message. It's like the card companies say, 'We give up, you think
of something. It's not worth us getting involved.'"[1]

That may be true for a card company, but we can assure you that it's well worth it for
you to get involved in understanding your own social life. After all, family and friends
sustain us. They shape our sense of identity. They provide us with shared understanding

and shared norms. Ultimately, our friends and family give us a sense of belonging. And this "belonging" is vital to our marriage. Their social support sustains our marriage. And this page of your SYMBIS+ Report is dedicated to helping you explore how you can leverage your social life to do just that. With its straightforward design, this page may be the most intuitive or simple to process, but it may also be one of the most eye-opening.

CONTENTMENT WITH FAMILY RELATIONSHIPS

Whether we admit it or not, all of us are indelibly shaped by family. In fact, most of what we think, say, and do—for better or worse—is a response to the home we came from. As psychiatrist Theodore Lidz points out in his book *The Person*, "It is in the family that patterns of emotional reactivity develop and interpersonal relationships are established that pattern and color all subsequent relationships."

Experts on the family consistently point to two areas where our family's power to shape us is most present: family rules and family roles.

Family Rules

Every family has its own unique set of unspoken rules. For example, one family may operate by the rule that everyone should get a graduate education. It isn't discussed; it is simply expected. Another family may live by the idea that real achievement is succeeding in the business without formal training.

What about you? What unspoken rules did your family live by? Take a moment to think about this. The following sentence stems can help you uncover these rules. Simply complete them by writing the first thing that pops into your head:

Men should . . . _____

Women should . . . _____

Success is . . . _____

The most important thing is . . . _____

Life is . . . _____

The point of uncovering your family's unspoken rules is to evaluate them from your personal perspective. Do you agree with them? Why or why not?

How we behave has a lot to do with our family constellation—whether we are oldest or youngest, male or female, and so on. Our birth order shapes our perspectives, for example, maybe even our career path.

Your Family Role

What part did you play in your family's drama? Consider the following roles to help you more accurately pinpoint your part:

- Problem solver
- Healer
- Victim

- Rescuer
- Comedian
- Mediator

- Confronter
- Secret keeper
- Other

You may also find it helpful to identify other family members' roles as well. Doing so will help you more clearly define your role. So review the list again and try to determine what role each member of your family played. By identifying your role in the family, you will become more empowered to fulfill it if you choose or to opt for a healthier pattern if need be.

Discuss with your spouse the role you played (and may continue to play) in your family. How has it shaped your role in your marriage?

How do your two roles from your separate families interact with each other in your marriage?

MY RELATIONSHIP WITH MY IN-LAWS

In-law issues may be grist for the mill for comedians, but in real life they are no laughing matter. Whether you adore your partner's parents or barely tolerate your in-laws, your rapport with them is worth the effort it takes to make the relationship as healthy and happy as possible.

Family Matters

Regardless of how well you are currently relating to your in-laws, you're likely to find this little exercise helpful. Why? Because it will cause you to reflect on your role with your in-laws and it will generate a beneficial discussion with your spouse.

I don't blame my partner for my in-laws' behavior.

STRONGLY DISAGREE									STRONGLY AGREE
1	2	3	4	5	6	7	8	9	10

Explain/example: _____

_____

I don't escalate in-law problems.

STRONGLY DISAGREE									STRONGLY AGREE
1	2	3	4	5	6	7	8	9	10

Explain/example: _____

_____

My expectations regarding my in-laws are reasonable.

STRONGLY DISAGREE									STRONGLY AGREE
1	2	3	4	5	6	7	8	9	10

Explain/example: _____

_____

I make my in-laws feel welcome and needed.

STRONGLY DISAGREE								STRONGLY AGREE	
1	2	3	4	5	6	7	8	9	10

Explain/example: _____

_____

I take the high ground with my in-laws.

STRONGLY DISAGREE								STRONGLY AGREE	
1	2	3	4	5	6	7	8	9	10

Explain/example: _____

_____

I give my in-laws the benefit of the doubt.

STRONGLY DISAGREE								STRONGLY AGREE	
1	2	3	4	5	6	7	8	9	10

Explain/example: _____

_____

I take an interest in my in-laws' life.

STRONGLY DISAGREE								STRONGLY AGREE	
1	2	3	4	5	6	7	8	9	10

Explain/example: _____

_____

I initiate fun activities with my in-laws.

STRONGLY DISAGREE   STRONGLY AGREE

| 1 | 2 | 3 | 4 | 5 | 6 | 7 | 8 | 9 | 10 |

Explain/example: _____

_____

_____

We get it. You married your spouse, not their parents. But you can make your shared life brighter by forging positive bonds with them. So as you review this exercise together, consider practical action steps both of you can take to see that happen.

PRIORITIZING TIME WITH MUTUAL FRIENDS

What most people call their "circle of friends" more closely resembles a triangle. Generally speaking, most of us have between five hundred and twenty-five-hundred acquaintances each year, representing the base of the triangle. Then there are the twenty to one hundred "core friends" in the middle. These we know by first name, and we see them somewhat regularly. At the top of the triangle are one to seven intimate friends. These people are closely involved in our lives, and their names are likely engraved on our hearts.

But when it comes to marriage, it can be tough for some couples to find other "couple friends" where everyone feels a sense of connection. This is particularly true on the front end of marriage when each person is comfortable with their own network of friends. But even for couples who have been married for many years it can be a challenge.

Who do we consider our "couple friends"—those we both enjoy being with together?

Are we content with the number of couple friends we have?

Getting Social

If you are looking for ways to cultivate more friends you both can enjoy together, take a moment to jot down your answers to these questions:

For us to really be comfortable with another couple as friends, what do they need to be like?

_____

_____

_____

Are we willing to start a small group with other couples? Why or why not?

_____

_____

_____

What friends could we invite over or do something with as couples?

_____

_____

_____

SOCIAL SUPPORT FROM MY FAITH COMMUNITY

You've probably heard about the research showing that couples who share religious beliefs tend to enjoy stronger and happier marriages. In fact, numerous studies show that couples are substantially more likely to report being happy in their relationship when both partners attend church regularly than when neither partner does. In fact, spouses who attend church together are about 9 percentage points more likely to say they are "very happy" or "extremely happy" than husbands and wives who do not.[2]

Whether you are religious or not, consider this last portion of your SYMBIS+ page, and complete this exercise to explore how the research around personal faith can inform how you approach it, or how you don't, in your marriage.

Exploring Faith and Happiness

So, what accounts for the stabilizing power of religion when it comes to your marriage? Several theories have been offered by Harvard professor Tyler VanderWeele to explain how faith is linked to happier couples.[3] Do you agree?

☐ **Yes** ☐ **No**　Religious teachings often indicate that marriage is something sacred—that an important bond is created in the exchange of marriage vows. Attending religious services reinforces that message.

Why or why not?_____

_____

_____

☐ **Yes** ☐ **No**　Religious teachings discourage divorce to varying degrees across religious traditions, which may lead to lower rates of divorce; moreover, religious traditions often have strong teachings against adultery, which is one of the strongest predictors of divorce.

Why or why not?_____

_____

_____

☐ **Yes** ☐ **No**　Religious teachings often place a strong emphasis on love and on putting the needs of others above one's own. This may improve the quality of married life and lower the likelihood of divorce.

Why or why not?_____

_____

_____

☐ **Yes** ☐ **No** Religious institutions often provide various types of family support, including a place for families to get to know one another and develop relationships, programs for children, marital and premarital counseling, and retreats and workshops focused on building a good marriage. Religious communities can provide important social support to foster marital health.

Why or why not?_____

_____

_____

 What is one thing you would like to tweak or do differently in your marriage as it relates to social support from a faith community?

Chapter 5

FINANCES

Gain all you can, save all you can, and give all you can.

—John Wesley

"There are some things money can't buy," says Harvard law professor Michael J. Sandel, "but these days, not much." Almost everything is up for sale, and if you have enough funds, you can buy what you want. Sandel lists the following examples in his book *What Money Can't Buy*:

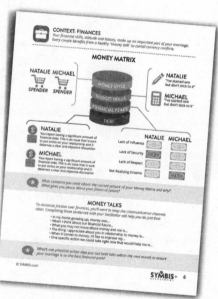

- *The right to jump to the head of the line at Universal Studios: $149.* Vacationers at Universal Studios can buy a special Front of Line Pass that allows them to cut to the front for all rides, shows, and attractions.
- *A prison-cell upgrade: $90 a night.* In some cities nonviolent offenders can pay for a clean, quiet jail cell, without any nonpaying prisoners to disturb them.
- *The right to shoot an endangered black rhino: $250,000.* South Africa has begun letting some ranchers sell hunters the right to kill a limited number of rhinos to give the ranchers an incentive to raise and protect the endangered species.
- *Access to the carpool lane while driving solo: about $8.* Some cities try to ease traffic congestion by letting solo drivers pay to drive in carpool lanes.

35

- *Your doctor's cellphone number: $1,500 and up per year.* A growing number of "concierge" doctors offer cellphone access and same-day appointments.[1]

The list goes on. No doubt about it, money talks. But as the Beatles said: money can't buy you love. You can't purchase an ideal or perfect marriage. In fact, money sometimes causes more conflict than it cures.

Research reveals that money is the single most difficult topic of conversation for couples—beating out other hot-button topics like politics. You've probably heard that finances cause more friction in marriage than any other topic. And it's true. Not only is it a difficult topic for many couples, but it sparks far too much conflict. According to a survey conducted by the American Institute of CPAs, financial matters trigger an average of three arguments per month for married couples. That rises to four finance-related fights per month for married couples aged forty-five to fifty-four. The most common source of financial contention? Disagreement over what's a "want" and what's a "need."

> It's good to have money and the things that money can buy, but it's good, too, to check up once in a while and make sure that you haven't lost the things that money can't buy.
>
> —George Lorimer

Regardless, every marriage expert agrees that couples of all ages need to open up the channels of communication surrounding money and marriage. And that's exactly what this page of your SYMBIS+ Report is dedicated to doing.

What we call your Money Matrix is made up of four important components: money style, budget skills, financial fears, and debt. This chapter will help you explore each of them without the risk of friction. So relax. This will be easier than you think—and more importantly, it will help you be able to reiterate what our friend and financial expert Ron Blue so often says: Money talks and so can we.

MONEY STYLE

As you can see on your report, each of you is identified as either a "saver" or a "spender." You know the difference. The person who knows to the dollar how much money is in their wallet or purse at any given moment or keeps track of how much they spend and where they spend it is probably a saver. The person who can't imagine life without that new pair of Nikes and doesn't have a clue what they spent yesterday is probably a spender.

One is not better or worse than the other. There are pros and cons to both sides. Spenders tend to be generous and giving, but they can also make impulsive decisions and end up with nothing to show for their hard work. Savers, on the other hand, tend to be naturally more responsible and can delay their gratification, but they can also become stingy. We'll say it again: one is not better than the other. And truth be told, most of us probably fall near the middle of the saving/spending continuum even though we lean in one of these two directions.

Saving versus Spending

Place a dollar sign on the continuum where you think you most accurately land:

SAVER ⬅️ ➡️ SPENDER

Why?_____

_____

_____

Now place a dollar sign on the continuum where you think your spouse most accurately lands:

SAVER ⬅️ ➡️ SPENDER

Why?_____

_____

_____

Compare notes with your partner and be sure to keep a grace-filled and receptive attitude. Remember, one is not better than the other.

BUDGET SKILLS

If you live by a budget religiously and you're both motivated and committed to working that budget to achieve your financial goals, congratulations! You are in the minority of couples and you can skip this little section of the chapter without an ounce of guilt. So go ahead. Move on to the Financial Fears section.

Okay. Now that those nerds have moved onto the next section let's talk truth for the rest of us. The word *budget* is cringeworthy to most of us. Why? It forces us to think twice about that set of golf clubs we've got our eye on or the new granite countertops we'd like to get. Budgeting, for many of us, feels like a deterrent to the things we want. Not surprisingly, two-thirds of Americans don't bother creating one. Of course, it's understandable. First of all, budgets involve math—something most of us were happy to put behind us once we left school. On top of that unpleasantness, a budget requires determination. Why? Because you have to stick to it. Paging Dr. Discipline.

Your emotional brain responds to the word *budget* the same way it responds to the word *diet*. They both conjure up deprivation, suffering, dread, and disappointment. Just like a diet gets us focused on what we can't eat, a budget can get us thinking about what we can't have, whether it's a new phone or a date night. Budgets imply scarcity.

But it doesn't have to be that way. When you think about it, a budget is simply a spending plan, a tool to help you achieve your goals and dreams.

Our Money Motivators

Think about the things you most value and enjoy. Get specific about those things. It might be touring Argentina, hosting a fancy dinner party on New Year's, giving a month's salary to Habitat for Humanity, taking piano lessons, learning to sail, or whatever. Your goal may be to pay off your credit card debt and enjoy the feeling of being debt-free. The idea is to identify two or three things you would really like to do if you had the money. Don't get hung up on making these your ultimate goals. They are just things that come to mind right now—you can always change them later.

Goal #1: _____
_____

Goal #2: _____
_____

Goal #3: _____
_____

Now compare your pie chart with your partner's and see if you can reach a general agreement on how you'd ideally like to see this look together.

These goals are your financial motivators. If it helps, find a photo or picture that represents each one of your goals and place it someplace where you'll see it often. Keeping your motivator top of mind is important when it comes to the psychology of executing your financial plan.

Next, simply make a personal pie chart showing how you think your yearly income should be allocated. Here's an example, but feel free to add different categories to your own:

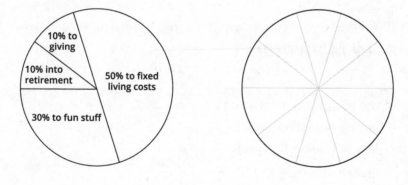

As for the actual nuts and bolts of setting up a realistic and livable budget, you probably already know what's required. But here's a great starter list form our friend Dave Ramsey:

- Write down your total income for the month. This is your total take-home (after tax) pay for both you and, if you're married, your spouse. Don't forget to include everything—full-time jobs, second jobs, freelance pay, Social Security checks, and any other ongoing sources of income.
- List all your expenses. Think about your regular bills (mortgage, electricity, etc.) and your irregular bills (quarterly payments such as insurance or HOA) that are due for the upcoming month. After that, total your other costs, like food, gas, entertainment, savings, and giving. Every dollar you spend should be accounted for.
- Subtract expenses from income to equal zero. This is called a zero-based budget, meaning your income minus your expenses should equal zero. If you're over or under, check your math or simply return to the previous step and try again.
- Track your expenses throughout the month. Once you start the budget, you'll still need to stay on top of your expenses. This last step can be the toughest, but Dave has made it easier than ever with a tool called EveryDollar. It's extremely easy and effective. Check it out at EveryDollar.com.

One more thought about budgets. Most of us pay for everything with a credit or debit card, which makes it a lot easier to underestimate our spending. A study from MIT, entitled "Always Leave Home without It," found that subjects were willing to spend 64 percent more on a pair of basketball tickets when using a credit card over cash.[2] Cash makes the purchase more tangible, forcing you to think twice about your spending.

 Are you willing to forgo using credit cards as an experiment for a year? Why or why not?

FINANCIAL FEARS

"My life has been filled with terrible misfortunes," said Mark Twain, "most of which have never happened." Love that quote. Isn't it true? So often we worry about things we can't control to begin with and that more than likely will never come to pass. And when it comes to our financial fears in marriage, it really doesn't matter whether they are grounded in reality or not. They're still real to us. They may be the result of our upbringing, a negative experience we've had, behaviors we've witnessed from our spouse, or some other factor.

Your SYMBIS+ Report page identifies you as having one of the following personal financial fears:

1. Lack of Influence—not having a say in your financial approach
2. Lack of Security—not having enough to live on or enough for emergencies
3. Lack of Respect—not receiving respect from your partner on finances
4. Not Realizing Dreams—not being able to do what you want in the future

Of course, you may have more than one of these. The report simply identifies the one that rises to the top.

Exploring Our Financial Fears

Write the name of your financial fear here:

_____

_____

_____

Identify some feeling words that surround your fear:

_____

_____

Take a moment to ponder *why* this is your top financial fear. Where did it come from?

_____

_____

_____

How does your financial fear show itself? What do you imagine it looks like to your spouse?

_____

_____

_____

What is one practical action you could take to help you manage or feel better about your financial fear?

_____

_____

_____

What is one thing your spouse could say or do that would help you feel better about your financial fear? Why would this be helpful?

_____

_____

_____

 As you compare your answers for the above exercises, what is the biggest insight you gained about your spouse and their financial fear?

DEBT

The last piece of your personal Money Matrix focuses on debt. If you're debt-free, congratulations! We'll assume you've also mastered the fine art of living with a financial plan. Way to go!

Whether it's from school loans, car loans, credit cards, or something else, the vast majority of couples have debt. So what about the two of you? Would you like to live debt-free? Of course! Who wouldn't? And it's possible. How do we know? Because we've seen couples dig out of debt time and time again. In fact, every time we are on Dave Ramsey's national radio broadcast for an interview about one of our books, we always stick around to watch a real-life couple do a debt-free scream. It's incredible. Don't believe us? Just look up the videos online. You'll see countless couples who built a budget, stuck to it, and dug themselves completely out of debt to realize their financial goals and dreams.

> For where your treasure is, there your heart will be also.
> —Matthew 6:21

Whether you eventually sign up for the scream at Dave's radio studio or not, you can do the same thing. We urge you to get serious about your debt—especially if you're having a hard time keeping up with your payments. You need Financial Peace University. Dave Ramsey and his team have a proven system that we can't recommend highly enough. Learn more at DaveRamsey.com.

 Why are we not taking more concrete action to dig out of our debt? What's keeping us from getting into Financial Peace University?

MONEY TALKS

You've explored your Money Matrix on this page of your report, and at the bottom of the page is a short exercise for every couple—whether you are struggling with your finances or sitting on top of the world. Why? Because it will give you deeper insight into each other's money makeup and bring you closer together to better manage your money as a team.

Money Talks

While you may have talked through a couple of these with your SYMBIS Facilitator, consider each of these sentences and write out how you would complete them:

In my home growing up, money was:

_____

_____

_____

When I think about our financial future:

_____

_____

_____

What you may not know about money and me is:

_____

_____

_____

The thing I appreciate about you in relationship to money is:

_____

_____

_____

When it comes to money, I'd like to improve my:

_____

_____

_____

One specific action we could take right now that would help me is:

_____

_____

_____

Once you've completed your sentences, review them and compare them with your spouse's. Be sure to come into this conversation with a heart for understanding (not evaluating).

Chapter 6

EXPECTATIONS

To wish was to hope, and to hope was to expect.

—Jane Austen

What's the first word that comes to mind when you hear the name Albert Einstein? If you're like most people, it's *genius*. Einstein (1879–1955) was an intellectual giant who was awarded the Nobel Prize in Physics in 1921, and his scientific pursuits have since inspired countless novels, films, plays, and works of music. Library shelves and search engines groan under the sheer weight of the data, true and false, amassed about Einstein and his life.

In spite of his intellectual impact on the world, however, he wasn't all that smart when it came to marriage. By 1914, his marriage to his first wife of eleven years, Mileva Marić, was fast deteriorating. In an effort to keep the marriage going, Einstein proposed a list of marital expectations for Mileva.

The list includes daily laundry "kept in good order," "three meals regularly *in my room*," a desk maintained neatly "for my use only," and the demand that she quit talking or leave the room "if I request it."[1] Not surprisingly, the marriage ended in divorce. After all, who would feel comfortable with a spouse who literally writes up a list of "marital expectations"?

Before we are too quick to jump to judgment, however, we need to recognize that expectations—whether explicit or not—are an ongoing part of married life. In fact, all of us have a list of marital expectations. It's true. The list is simply unspoken and maybe even unconscious. But even so, we know when our spouse doesn't meet an expectation. We know when our spouse doesn't fulfill what we think they should do as our husband or wife.

It has been said that "expectations are premeditated resentments." Why? Because when we buy into a list of unspoken or unconscious expectations around our spouse, we are setting ourselves up for disappointment. And disappointments, when they mount up, turn into resentments over our spouse's failure to fulfill our unspoken expectations. In actuality, we end up blaming our spouse for things they don't even know about. That's why this page of your SYMBIS+ Report is dedicated to making unconscious role expectations conscious. It's dedicated to giving voice to unspoken expectations that might never be discussed otherwise.

Getting Honest about Unspoken Expectations

To get the most out of this page of your SYMBIS+ Report, it's important to have an attitude that conveys you accept the fact that you actually do have unspoken expectations around your spouse.

Honestly note where you fall on this scale and explain your reasoning:

"I ALWAYS MAKE MY EXPECTATIONS EXPLICIT."   **"I'M SURE I HAVE UNSPOKEN EXPECTATIONS."**

1	2	3	4	5	6	7	8	9	10

Why? _____

_____

_____

_____

UNSPOKEN EXPECTATIONS CAN LEAD TO MAGICAL THINKING

Developmental psychologist Jean Piaget noted that young children have difficulty distinguishing between the subjective worlds in their heads and the outer, objective world. According to Piaget, children sometimes believe that their thoughts can directly cause things to happen. They may believe, for example, that their angry feelings about their little brother can cause him to fall down the stairs. Piaget referred to this as *magical thinking* and suggested that we all outgrow it by around age seven.

But do we? We've seen many normal adults continue to engage in various forms of magical thinking when it comes to their spouse. "If he really loved me, I wouldn't have to tell him how I feel because he'd already know." Or, "Why does she need me to constantly tell her how much I love her when my actions speak for themselves?"

Mind Reading

This exercise will help you avoid magical thinking with each other. How? By helping you make your thinking more explicit. In fact, it will help you to avoid the inevitable mind reading that most couples seem to do, whether they know it or not.

This exercise, by the way, is one that you can do many times—in moments when you need to the most. It will take about ten minutes.

Normally, trying to "mind read" what your partner is thinking is an unhealthy undertaking because it will lead you to jump to irrational conclusions. That's why in this exercise you will actually assess the accuracy of your assumptions before acting on them.

The next time you sense that your partner is upset with you, pause for a moment and say, "I want to read your mind." Then tell your spouse what you think they were saying to themselves.

For example, "I think you're mad about the way I left the bed this morning," or "I think you're upset because I wanted to watch TV instead of take a walk."

Then say, "How accurate am I?"

Your partner can then rate how accurate you are on a percentage scale. For example, your partner might say, "That's about 20 percent accurate," or "That's 100 percent accurate."

This simple exercise can be done anytime you sense that your partner is upset, and you'd like to know if you are right about the reasons for it. Every couple mind reads every day. This exercise just makes that habit up front and more useful and keeps you from the downfalls of magical thinking that fuel misguided expectations.

To get the feel of how this exercise works, consider how your partner was thinking or feeling about something in your relationship that happened within the last couple of days. Of course, this exercise is most helpful when used in the present tense (while you are in the midst of an experience), but to get the hang of it you'll bring up something that has already happened—something that you never really processed but that you made assumptions about (e.g., you think they were upset when you didn't show up on time). Once you have that instance in mind, complete this sentence:

I think you were . . .

_____

_____

_____

Now ask your spouse how accurate you are in this assumption and note it on the following scale:

COMPLETELY INACCURATE									RIGHT ON THE MONEY
1	2	3	4	5	6	7	8	9	10

Again, the point of this simple exercise is to curtail your natural inclination to "mind read" by making your assumptions and expectations known. You'll be amazed how handy this can be in the midst of an intense conversation.

What do you think of the mind reading exercise? Do you think we can put this into practice the next time it might be helpful? What can we do to help each other remember this exercise in the moment?

GREAT EXPECTATIONS

Pete Rose, the famous baseball player, was being interviewed in spring training the year he was about to break Ty Cobb's all-time hits record. A reporter asked, "Pete, you only need seventy-eight hits to break the record. How many at-bats do you think you'll need to get the seventy-eight hits?" Without hesitation, Pete just stared at the reporter and very matter-of-factly said, "Seventy-eight." The reporter yelled back, "Ah, come on Pete, you don't expect to get seventy-eight hits in seventy-eight at-bats, do you?"

Mr. Rose calmly shared his philosophy with the reporters who were anxiously awaiting his reply to this seemingly boastful claim. "Every time I step up to the plate, I expect to get a hit! If I don't expect to get a hit, I have no right to step in the batter's box in the first place! If I go up hoping to get a hit," he continued, "then I probably don't have a prayer to get a hit. It is a positive expectation that has gotten me all of the hits in the first place."

> Life is so constructed, that the event does not, cannot, will not, match the expectation.
> —Charlotte Brontë

Positive Expectation—this page of your SYMBIS+ Report reveals a list of expectations the two of you already agree on. Fantastic! But if you're like most couples, the page also reveals a list of expectations where the two of you aren't exactly in sync. Exploring these expectations can help you get more in tune with each other.

Getting in Sync

Review the items under the second green ribbon on your report. You may have just a small handful of items here or more than a dozen. Write down three of them and what you would like to see happen.

Expectation to resolve: _____

What you'd like to see happen:

_____

_____

Expectation to resolve: _____

What you'd like to see happen:

_____

_____

Expectation to resolve: _____

What you'd like to see happen:

_____

_____

 What is the biggest take-away each of you got from exploring this page of your report? What positive difference will it make in your marriage?

Chapter 7

REMARRIAGE AND BLENDING A FAMILY

We have been poisoned by fairy tales.

Anaïs Nin

NOTE: If one or both of you are remarried or blending a family, this page (7A) appears in your SYMBIS+ Report. If not, you can simply move on to the next chapter.

Shortly after our book *Saving Your Marriage Before It Starts* was first published, we began getting requests for information from couples who had become engaged after one or both of them were in a previous marriage that had ended either in death or divorce. These couples, on the brink of remarrying, knew there were issues and struggles ahead of them that were unique to their situation—compared to couples getting married for the first time.

After all, some of them had children they would be bringing with them into their new marriage. Others had baggage from a previous marriage; either they were enveloped by grief from the loss of a spouse or they felt burned by a spouse who had hurt them deeply. And still others were entering a second marriage with more than a little anxiety and wanted to be sure they did everything they could to ensure success the second time around.

At the urging of these couples, we began considering the needs of remarried couples. What we found compelled us to write another book: *Saving Your Second Marriage Before It Starts*. Seventy-five percent of those who divorce will marry again. Remarriage is nearly as common as first marriages, yet more than 60 percent of remarriages end in divorce. What's more, second marriages in which there are children in the family are twice as likely to end in divorce as remarriages in which there are no children.[1] But it was another single piece of information that really made our hearts sink: *Many remarried couples conclude within the first months that their new marriage is failing, when, in fact, studies have shown that the estimated time it takes to adapt to being a stepfamily ranges from two to seven years.*

Allow us to say it bluntly: Remarried couples face a rocky road. Experience, unfortunately, is not the best predictor of success when it comes to marriage. That's not to say that you are bound to have major difficulties. Not by a long shot. In fact, we know from research that you are already increasing your odds of success dramatically compared to other couples in a second marriage. How do we know? Because you sought out a SYMBIS+ Facilitator, you've taken the assessment, and you're working through this guidebook. That tells us you are doing everything you can to make your second marriage a first-class success.

RELATIONSHIP RESIDUE AND UNRESOLVED ISSUES

We all have unfinished business. The top two portions of this page of your SYMBIS+ Report highlight several of the most common issues. You've likely already reviewed these with your Facilitator. The following exercise will help you take that process even deeper.

Stepfamilies are the moral pioneers of contemporary family life, showing us all how to love and persevere in the face of loyalties that multiply and divide, but never fully converge.
William Doherty

Keeping the Slate Clean

Healthy marriages are honest. The partners reveal their hearts to each other with care and compassion—even thoughts and feelings and reflections about the first marriage. For the person in your marriage who has been married before (perhaps it's both of you), take a moment to complete each of these sentence stems:

The things that initially attracted me to my first spouse were . . .

_____

_____

I decided to marry my first spouse because . . .

_____

_____

My first spouse added positive value to our relationship by . . .

_____

_____

I personally contributed to the relationship's difficulties by . . .

_____

_____

I still feel angry about . . .

_____

_____

I still feel guilty about . . .

_____

_____

A lesson I learned about marriage that is helping me in my second marriage is . . .

_____

_____

What my first marriage taught me about myself is . . .

_____

_____

Once you have completed these sentence stems, discuss with your spouse. If both of you have been married before, you can take turns responding to each item. Keep in mind that the goal is to keep your marriage honest and caring by learning from your previous marriage.

 What is your biggest fear when it comes to blending your family at this point? Why?

BLENDING A FAMILY

Stepfamily expert Ron Deal compares bringing children into a second marriage to trying to put together a 3D jigsaw puzzle without a picture on the box cover to show what it's supposed to look like. Needless to say, it's complicated.

You've already noted with your Facilitator the half dozen issues on the bottom third of this page of your SYMBIS+ Report. You've identified some of the potential deficits you may have in the process of blending your families. The following exercise will help you capitalize on some of the strengths you bring to the mix.

Life in a Blender

Chances are that both of you are doing some extraordinarily positive and healthy things to make your home happy for both you and your children. Consider this list of important actions and attitudes, all qualities of a thriving blended family. Each of you can rate how you believe you are doing individually and as a couple when it comes to these items:

Being civil to ex-spouses

NOT DOING WELL   *DOING VERY WELL*

| 1 | 2 | 3 | 4 | 5 | 6 | 7 | 8 | 9 | 10 |

Having clarity on who disciplines children and when

NOT DOING WELL   *DOING VERY WELL*

| 1 | 2 | 3 | 4 | 5 | 6 | 7 | 8 | 9 | 10 |

Empathizing with and supporting the spouse in the stepparent role

NOT DOING WELL   *DOING VERY WELL*

| 1 | 2 | 3 | 4 | 5 | 6 | 7 | 8 | 9 | 10 |

Not trying to replace or replicate the missing parent

NOT DOING WELL   *DOING VERY WELL*

| 1 | 2 | 3 | 4 | 5 | 6 | 7 | 8 | 9 | 10 |

Giving the biological parent time alone with and without the children

NOT DOING WELL   *DOING VERY WELL*

| 1 | 2 | 3 | 4 | 5 | 6 | 7 | 8 | 9 | 10 |

Discussing openly and dealing with new or unexpected issues as they come up

NOT DOING WELL   *DOING VERY WELL*

| 1 | 2 | 3 | 4 | 5 | 6 | 7 | 8 | 9 | 10 |

Building new family traditions while including and respecting the old ones

NOT DOING WELL   *DOING VERY WELL*

| 1 | 2 | 3 | 4 | 5 | 6 | 7 | 8 | 9 | 10 |

Once you've taken the time to discuss these issues with each other, identify the top two or three that matter most to you. Next, make a game plan and set some achievable goals. What can you do in practical terms to improve these issues in your marriage?

Chapter 8

INDIVIDUAL DYNAMICS

There is little difference in people, but that little difference makes a big difference.

—W. Clement Stone

"Why in the world wouldn't you want to know this?" Les asked.

"Because some things are better left unknown," I replied.

"You're telling me that if you could have your personal DNA spelled out in detail for you, you wouldn't want to know?" he continued to poke. "I mean, you wouldn't want to know what traits you've inherited and what diseases you are most at risk for?"

"No. Not really."

"I don't get it—information is power. This information puts you in the driver's seat of understanding your own genotype."

"Well, for now, I feel more comfortable just being along for the ride."

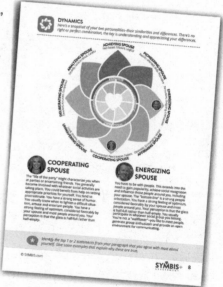

This animated exchange lasted a good thirty minutes. We had tucked into bed our two little boys and were enjoying the quiet of the evening, sitting in Les's study, when he said with enthusiasm, "Listen to this."

He began reading an article about one of *Time* magazine's "Inventions of the Year"—a retail DNA test that provides you with an online summary of your own genetic makeup (once you provide them with a saliva sample).

Les was gung-ho, ready to plunk down our hard-earned cash on a saliva kit that would tell him whether he was prone to Parkinson's disease, male pattern baldness, back pain, restless leg syndrome, and ninety-two other bits of biological information.

Me? Not so much. I'm content to not know—and I made that seemingly bewildering fact known to him.

"That's probably one of the things your DNA report would reveal."

"What?" I asked with genuine curiosity.

"Maybe it would show you why you're not more proactive and curious on these matters," Les said, just partly kidding. "Maybe it would show you why you tend to be more passive and why I'm more proactive."

"Actually, that's a report I *would* be interested in."

"What do you mean?" Les asked me.

"I'd like a report that reveals my personality traits and compares them with yours—to show us how our two personalities intermingle to shape our marriage relationship."

It was that conversation, years ago, that became part of the catalyst for launching the SYMBIS+ Assessment. We'd been researching and studying the topic for years. But in that moment, both of us instantly realized how valuable such an assessment could be, not only to our own relationship but to so many others. After all, if you could accurately understand how your spouse is hardwired for love, not to mention your own hardwiring,

> Marriage is the alliance of two people, one of whom never remembers birthdays and the other who never forgets them.
> —Ogden Nash

wouldn't it almost instantly curb the number of conflicts you encounter? Of course! Wouldn't it create quicker and easier ways to understand one another and bring you closer together? Absolutely!

That's why we have been excited for you to get to this chapter of this guidebook. You've likely already unpacked this important page of your report with your SYMBIS Facilitator, and this chapter will help you contextualize it even more to your marriage.

THERE'S NOBODY JUST LIKE YOU

Your DNA—that molecule found in almost every cell of your body—not only encodes the basic blueprint for your biological traits and predispositions, but also includes much of the encoding for your basic personality. And understanding your personality, as well as your partner's, is central to enjoying lifelong love. Why? Because it's the most efficient and effective road to mutual empathy. The more each of you can accurately see the world from each other's perspectives, the easier and more loving your relationship becomes.

Did you know that we humans have about 99.9 percent of our DNA in common? This means that only 0.1 percent of each person's DNA is unique. Yet that minuscule proportion of our DNA is enough to create seeming chasms of dissimilarity between us. Does it have a name? Sure. Some call it your temperament. Some call it your nature or character. Mystics call it your spirit while others call it your personality. Whatever you call it, we all have it. Like a fingerprint, that tiny genetic difference makes each one of us totally and completely one of a kind.

Your Two Personalities

You've already read the paragraph describing your personality on this page. With the assistance of your Facilitator you may have highlighted the things you resonate with most and crossed out anything you disagree with.

After doing so, how well do you think this paragraph starts to describe your personality?

Honestly note where you fall on this scale and explain your reasoning:

NOT ACCURATE AT ALL   VERY ACCURATE

| 1 | 2 | 3 | 4 | 5 | 6 | 7 | 8 | 9 | 10 |

Why? _____

_____

_____

Now, consider your spouse's personality paragraph. Note where you fall on this scale and explain your reasoning:

DOES NOT DESCRIBE MY SPOUSE   ACCURATELY DESCRIBES MY SPOUSE

| 1 | 2 | 3 | 4 | 5 | 6 | 7 | 8 | 9 | 10 |

Why? _____

_____

_____

What is it about your two personalities that makes it easy and what makes it difficult to see the world from each other's perspectives?

PROJECT VERSUS PEOPLE

We happen to live about four blocks from the Nordstrom headquarters and flagship department store in downtown Seattle. On more than one occasion we have had the privilege of speaking in the boardroom of this company to some of the executives and employees. And as you walk through the various floors of office suites, you can't help but notice the same sign hanging in different places. It says: "The only difference between stores is the way they treat their customers."

Now, if you've done much shopping at Nordstrom, you know exactly what that sign means. You see, most stores advertise the quality of their merchandise or the wide selection of their goods. But not Nordstrom. The difference between Nordstrom and most other stores is that other stores are project oriented—Nordstrom is people oriented. Their employees are trained to respond quickly and kindly to customer complaints. As a result, according to business consultant Nancy Austin, "Nordstrom doesn't have customers; it has fans."

Now that's all good and well, you might be saying, but there have to be some people in the organization who focus on the bottom line more than the customers. And you're right. These employees don't interface much with the customers. Their job is to focus on product quality and inventory. They look at everything from the way the lights hit a display of shoes to the way sweaters are folded and arranged. They are aware of traffic flow within the store and they know how long a product can sit before being discounted. And, fact is, Nordstrom couldn't survive without both groups. No effective organization can. We need both people-oriented and task-oriented individuals. One is not better than the other. Just different.

Task or People Oriented?

Within the personality pinwheel on your report, you've likely already discovered two circles. The outer circle notes "Task Oriented" on the top and "People Oriented" on the bottom. Note which camp you fall into (or maybe you're right on the dividing line).

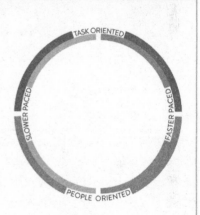

The following list contrasts these two groups. Each of you can place your initials next to three qualities you identify with most. You may choose from either side, but you must choose three qualities each.

TASK ORIENTED	PEOPLE ORIENTED
Driven	Nurturing
Measurable goals	Heartfelt connections
Work from a to-do list ⅃	What to-do list?
Concentrated and focused	Welcome interruptions ⅃
Delay gratification	Procrastinate
Make others feel nervous	Make others feel comfortable
"Fish or cut bait"	"Easy come, easy go"

As you know, there are no right or wrong answers. Fifty percent of the population falls into each side of this continuum—some people more extreme than others. Take a moment to note one or two real-life, concrete examples that illustrate any of your three characteristics:

_____

_____

_____

 How does your approach—whether it's task-oriented, people-oriented, or both—impact your relationship (for good or ill)? No need to size up your spouse. Simply talk about yourself (for now).

FAST VERSUS SLOW

On the third Monday of every April since 1897, the world's oldest annual marathon takes place in Boston, Massachusetts. Today an average of twenty-thousand registered participants wind through the 26.2 miles of streets to the finish line at Copley Square. And it's there that you'll find, year-round, a bronze statue of two animals: a tortoise and a hare.

Of course, they are there to remind everyone of Aesop's legendary fable: One day a hare saw a tortoise walking slowly along and began to laugh and mock him. The hare challenged the tortoise to a race and the tortoise accepted. They agreed on a route and started the race. The hare shot ahead and ran briskly for some time. Then, seeing that he was far ahead of the tortoise, he thought he'd sit under a tree and relax before continuing the race. He soon fell asleep. When the hare awoke, however, he found that his competitor, crawling slowly but steadily, had already won the race.

The moral of the story? It depends on who you identify with most. If it's the tortoise, you'll say: "Slow and steady wins the race." But if it's the hare, you'll counter: "You snooze you lose."

So which one are you? The tortoise or the hare? Do you approach your day like a long marathon, slow and steady? Or do you jump into the rat race of your day like it's a sprint to the finish? Of course, your SYMBIS+ page contains the answer.

Slower or Faster Paced?

Now shift your attention to the *inner* circle on the personality pinwheel. Which camp do you fall into? Again, you may be somewhere in the middle. Each of you can place your initials next to three qualities you identify with most. You may choose from either side, but you must choose only three qualities each.

FAST PACED	SLOW PACED
Divide and conquer	Unite and concede
Impatient	Patient –
Raring to go	Ready to rest –
Excited and energetic	Steady and stable –
To the point –	Round about
"Don't just sit there, do something"	"Think before you act" –
"Early bird gets the worm"	"Slow growing trees bear the best fruit"

Again, there are no right or wrong answers. Take a moment to note one or two real-life, concrete examples that illustrate any of your three characteristics:

_____

_____

_____

How does your approach—whether it's fast or slow paced (or both)—impact your relationship? Again, there's no need to size up your spouse; just answer for yourself.

Chapter 9

RELATIONSHIP DYNAMICS

All weddings are similar, but every marriage is different.

—John Berger

A few years ago, we were speaking at a marriage seminar in Wichita, Kansas. We arrived late in the evening at our hotel, but the atmosphere in the lobby was electric. It was buzzing with people who seemed giddy with excitement.

As we made our way through the crowd to the registration desk, we asked the clerk about the activity. "We have some special guests with us tonight," he said calmly. We waited for him to reveal the secret, but it soon became obvious that he wasn't telling. With our hotel key in hand we once again surveyed the swarm of people across the lobby and realized that many of them were wearing T-shirts with the unmistakable tongue

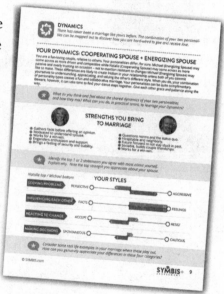

and lips logo of the Rolling Stones. And just at that moment, none other than aging rocker Mick Jagger himself stepped out of a stretch limo and strolled right by us and his adoring groupies to be whisked toward a private elevator.

As we rode up to our floor in a not-so-private elevator, fellow hotel guests were making a game of naming as many Rolling Stones songs as they could. "Satisfaction" followed quickly by "You Can't Always Get What You Want," "Start Me Up," and so on. Then somebody said, "Emotional Rescue."

"Sing it," someone urged.

"I'll be steadfast and true, I'll come to your emotional rescue," the tipsy guest warbled.

That's when the elevator doors opened for our floor. "I don't know the song," Leslie said, "but I know the feeling."

> Love is not blind—it sees more, not less. But because it sees more, it is willing to see less.
> —Julius Gordon

"What feeling?"

"The feeling of wanting you to come to my emotional rescue."

And who doesn't? After all, it's not just attraction that keeps a couple together. It's their mutual caretaking that sustains them. In fact, the ability to come to your partner's "emotional rescue" is the sure sign of empathy. Wouldn't you love to be able to do this for each other more consistently? Wouldn't you like your spouse to be at the ready whenever you need a bit of emotional soothing? Well, that's exactly what this page of your SYMBIS+ Report is designed to help with.

 Just for fun, think about the first date the two of you had. How did your unique personalities come through even as you were first getting to know each other?

YOUR DYNAMICS

Understanding your two unique personalities is simply a tool for helping you both get the love you want. By taking a deep look at your inner hardwiring (on the previous page of your report), we hope we've helped you enter each other's worlds—taking you a few steps closer to mutual empathy. But your SYMBIS+ Report can do better than simply giving you a snapshot of your two personalities. On this page of your report, it shows you how to leverage your unique dynamics together.

The Mix of Your Two Personalities

The top section of this page of your report contains a highly personalized paragraph. It describes the chemistry or the mix of your two personalities. Of course, you've already reviewed it with your Facilitator, but revisit it now and answer the following:

If you were reading this paragraph about a couple you didn't know, what would stand out most to you and why?

_____

_____

_____

Based on your two personalities, what is missing from this combo paragraph? In other words, if you were to add a sentence to the paragraph, what would it say?

_____

_____

_____

Based on this information, what's one practical and concrete action you can take within the next twenty-four hours to be a better spouse to your partner?

_____

_____

_____

STRENGTHS YOU BRING TO THE RELATIONSHIP

They call it the deadlift. The rules are simple: Lift a loaded barbell off the ground to the level of the hips, perpendicular to the floor, before placing it back on the ground. The world record? It's held by a twenty-eight-year old strongman named Eddie Hall who lifted 1,103 pounds. Incredible, right?

We are all impressed by feats of strength. And when it comes to personality strengths and what people bring into their relationships it's spectacular. Your strengths, combined with your spouse's, make for a formidable bond that enables the two of you to power through tough times and go the distance. Your strengths also add to the fun and love you experience in your marriage.

Exploring Your Spouse's Strengths

Hopefully, you've already explored the five strengths noted on this page of your SYMBIS+ Report. You've noted the top couple of strengths each of you brings to your relationship. This exercise takes it a step further and helps you explore the strengths you see in your spouse—and the strengths your spouse sees in you.

On the next page is a list of dozens of potential strengths.

1. Peruse this list and circle what you perceive to be the top fifteen or so strengths of your spouse. Go with your first impression, for the most part. It's okay to have more than fifteen.

2. Next, review your list of your spouse's strengths and narrow it down to ten. Give yourself some time to think of examples of when your spouse exhibits these strengths.

3. Finally, share your list of the top ten strengths and explain why you chose each one. Use this as an opportunity to shower your spouse with affirmation and appreciation.

- AMBITIOUS
- MOTIVATED
- CANDID
- COOPERATIVE ✓
- DECISIVE
- DEVOTED ✓
- DETERMINED ✓
- ENTHUSIASTIC ✓
- EXPERIENCED
- FLEXIBLE
- FOCUSED
- HARD-WORKING ✓
- INVOLVED
- MATURE
- OPEN-MINDED
- PRACTICAL
- PUNCTUAL ✓ lol
- REALISTIC
- RELIABLE ✓
- RESPECTFUL

- RESPONSIBLE ✓
- RESPONSIVE
- SEASONED
- SELF-CONFIDENT ✓
- SELF-DIRECTED
- SELF-DISCIPLINED
- WILLING
- ARTICULATE
- CALM
- CAPABLE
- CHARISMATIC
- CLEAR-HEADED
- CONSIDERATE ✓
- CREATIVE
- CURIOUS
- EFFICIENT
- EMPATHETIC
- FLEXIBLE
- FORTHRIGHT
- HELPFUL

- HONEST
- IMAGINATIVE
- INDEPENDENT
- INNOVATIVE
- INSIGHTFUL
- INTUITIVE
- KIND
- METHODICAL
- METICULOUS
- NEAT
- OBJECTIVE
- ORGANIZED
- PAINSTAKING
- PASSIONATE
- PATIENT
- PERCEPTIVE ?
- PERSUASIVE
- PRUDENT
- RESOURCEFUL
- SOCIABLE ✓

- SYSTEMATIC
- THOROUGH
- WELL-ROUNDED
- COMPETITIVE
- OUTSPOKEN
- COMMUNICATIVE
- HUMBLE
- NATURAL LEADER
- TEAM PLAYER
- ADAPTABLE
- DILIGENT
- ENERGETIC
- FRANK ✓
- INVENTIVE
- POLITE
- PRO-ACTIVE
- SENSIBLE
- SINCERE
- THOUGHTFUL ✓
- VERSATILE

 How do you feel after hearing about all the qualities your spouse appreciates in you? And how did it feel to highlight your spouse's strengths? Why do you think spouses don't do this more often?

YOUR STYLES

Whenever we teach counseling students at our university, we always use a simple metaphor to make the distinction between sympathy and empathy. It's an important distinction because professional counselors could never survive on mere sympathy. If they don't get a lock on empathy while working with their clients, their careers will be short-lived.

We tell our students that sympathy is standing on the shore and throwing a life-ring out to a person who is struggling in the water. Every decent human being would do this. It flows with our adrenaline.

Empathy is much riskier. Empathy is diving into the water and thrashing around in the cold waves with that person to bring them to safety. Not everyone does that. In fact, it's so rare that we call the people who do "heroes." We put their picture in the paper and sometimes even have a parade.

Well, it can be just as heroic when we do practice empathy in our own marriage. Why? Because empathy *is* risky. It will change you. Once you immerse yourself into your partner's predicament or situation (with your head and heart), you won't look at your partner the same way. You'll have a new perspective that makes you more patient, more grace-giving, and more caring.

This gift of empathy for each other is particularly evident (or not) in four areas of married life: (1) solving problems together, (2) influencing each other, (3) reacting to change, and (4) making decisions. The lower portion of this page of your SYMBIS+ Report is dedicated to helping you see how you and your spouse tend to behave (based on the hardwiring of your personalities) in these areas.

SOLVING PROBLEMS

You've already discovered where you land on the problem-solving continuum. You are either more reflective or more aggressive when it comes to solving problems. What you may not know is how much this issue is tied to time. Why? Because the closer you are to the "Aggressive" end of the continuum, the greater the sense of *urgency* you feel. You don't like wasting time. When you face a problem, you don't put it off. You tackle it now! You're all about speed. This means that if both of you are aggressive problem solvers, you might be knocking down problems left and right. Good for you. But that doesn't mean you don't have friction over problem solving. It just means you're both urgent. You can still disagree on *how* a particular problem should be solved. And it almost goes without saying: nobody has called you out for being especially impatient.

If you are on the "Reflective" end of the problem-solving continuum, you take your time. No need to be in a rush. You know that sometimes, given enough time, problems simply take care of themselves. Living your life with a sense of urgency makes little sense to you. And if you're married to a person who shares this part of your personality, you offer each other an abundance of patience.

Of course, it's not at all unlikely that the two of you fall on different sides of the continuum. The reflective problem solver's relaxed approach obviously can frustrate an aggressive partner. After all, the reflective problem solver is far more careful and considerate, wanting to avoid conflict and steer clear of any tension. This approach comes off as unmotivated and indecisive to an aggressive spouse. You get the picture. And so does any reflective problem solver whose partner is a forceful problem solver.

The Urgency Factor

Consider a couple of relatively recent problems the two of you have had to solve together—problems whose solutions you didn't see from the same perspective, at least initially. It may have had something to do with a child's schooling, maintenance on your car, a house repair issue, etc. The problem doesn't really matter. Just identify a couple of times when the two of you didn't see a problem from the same side and note them below.

Problem to be solved #1:

_____

_____

_____

Now note where each of you would fall on this continuum (for this specific problem):

LET'S GIVE IT
SOME TIME ⬅▬▬▬▬▬▬▬▬➡ LET'S DO IT NOW

Problem to be solved #2:

_____

_____

_____

Note where each of you would fall on this continuum (for this specific problem):

LET'S GIVE IT
SOME TIME ⬅ ▬▬▬▬▬▬▬▬▬▬▬▬ ➡ LET'S DO IT NOW

As you consider these two problems you recently solved together, think about how the "urgency factor" or lack thereof, influenced your ability to get to a solution. Did it help or hinder and why? Also, how can seeing problem-solving from your spouse's point of view give you more empathy for them the next time you face a problem?

INFLUENCING EACH OTHER

Every day in nearly every way we are attempting to influence one another. Our conversations are consumed by it: "You're not going to wear that, are you?" "How can you support a candidate who has this kind of a record?" "Did you know that men who don't have a physical checkup at your age are twice as likely to have a medical problem within the next five years?" "I know you don't like lemons, but you're going to love this lemon cake—I just know it."

Our attempts to influence each other, on the mundane as well as the major issues of life, are unending. Influencing each other to do this or that or not to do something at all takes up an untold portion of your daily conversations. And knowing whether your spouse is influenced more powerfully by feelings or by facts can go a long way in making your marriage run more smoothly. Why? Because, once again, it deepens your capacity to empathize with your spouse.

 What is a concrete example from your relationship where this continuum of "facts versus feelings" plays out?

Let's clear something up just in case it's roaming around in your head. People don't choose to be influenced by facts or by feelings, just as they don't choose how short or how tall they are. How we are influenced is part of our makeup. The same is true for all of these dimensions we are exploring in this section. They are part of our DNA.

REACTING TO CHANGE

Whether you are accepting of change or resistant to it, every married couple needs to learn how to change in order to grow. If we don't, we get stuck. In his book *Teaching the Elephant to Dance*, James Belasco describes how trainers shackle young elephants with heavy chains to deeply embedded stakes, which is how they learn to stay in place. Older, powerful elephants never try to leave—even though they have the strength to pull the stake and walk away. Their conditioning has limited their movements. With only a small metal bracelet around their foot, they stand in place.

Like powerful elephants, we are sometimes bound by previously conditioned restraints. The statement "We have always done it this way" can be as limiting to a couple's progress as the unattached chain around an elephant's foot. After all, sometimes change is necessary. It's healthy. A promotion or a new job requires change. As does a chance for your child to excel by going to a different school. Progress mandates change. To let a good opportunity pass you by will burn to ashes all potential for realizing a dream.

A Change Might Do Us Good

In this simple exercise, we want you to consider two practical and health-giving changes that you think would benefit your relationship. It might be something like instituting a weekly date night or turning your phones off at dinner. Or maybe even having dinner around the table a few nights a week. It might be exercising together, attending a marriage workshop, beginning a couples' small group, or starting a new hobby. The list is endless.

Simply note two practical, positive, and specific changes you'd like to make to benefit your relationship.

Change #1:

_____

_____

_____

What is keeping us from making this change starting this week? And how will our personalities, our hardwiring, help or hinder this change?

_____

_____

_____

Change #2:

_____

_____

_____

What is keeping us from making this change starting this week? And how will our personalities, our hardwiring, help or hinder this change?

_____

_____

_____

 As you consider the healthy changes you'd both like to make—changes that will strengthen your relationship—which one would you like to execute first? What will each of you do this very day to make the change a reality?

MAKING DECISIONS

Several years ago, when a Realtor was showing us properties around Seattle, we came upon a lot near a golf course that we both fell in love with. There were nature trails nearby, a glimpse of the mountains. It was gorgeous. Les was ready to make an offer. Not me. I loved the property, but I needed to think about how living there would impact what schools my boys went to, and where I would be in relationship to my friends.

"Don't you have to think this stuff through?" I asked Les.

"I know we can make it work," he replied. "It's farther from the airport, but where else are you going to find a lot like this? It's great. I say we buy it before somebody else does."

"I just don't know. I love the lot, but it may change the quality of life for our boys. They won't get to go to Kings, or if they do it would be a huge commute each day for them. And it will change our social circle. We'd have to go to a different church."

You get the idea. I'm just more careful and cautious about decision making than Les is. He's more of a risk taker than me. He's also more unconventional, pioneering, and independent in his decision making. I'm more of a conformist, more likely to follow the rules and do the right thing the right way.

One way is not better than the other. Just different. But knowing how we are hardwired to make decisions can go a long way in helping us recognize and even celebrate our differences in this area.

Ultimately, when we become aware of our own personality makeup as well as our partner's (involving solving problems, making decisions, and all the rest), we open the way for more understanding, more acceptance, more affirmation and ultimately more empathy.

Seeing through Each Other's Eyes

First, close your eyes and see yourself, in your mind's eye, as your partner. Do your best to imagine what it would be like to live in their skin. Take a good sixty seconds to ponder this.

Next, consider a typical day and ask yourself the following questions. We've provided space under each one of them for you to jot a little note so that you can later compare your thoughts with your partner's.

On a typical day as your partner . . .

What time did you get up in the morning, and how did you sleep? What is your morning mood like and why?

_____

_____

How long would it take you to get ready for the day? Would you spend more or less time in front of the mirror? What would you wear?

_____

_____

When would you leave the house, if you left at all? What would your activities throughout the day be?

_____

_____

What would you worry about in a typical day? What would be your likely stress points?

_____

_____

What would bring you the greatest joy or satisfaction during a typical day?

_____

_____

Would you have different financial responsibilities or pressures?

_____

_____

Would you eat differently? Exercise differently? Would you be more or less concerned about your physical appearance?

_____

_____

Would you feel more or less self-assured?

_____

_____

How would you feel toward the end of the day as you're getting ready for dinner? What would be on your mind?

_____

_____

And how would you feel about your partner (that would be you!)? What would you want most from your partner? How would you communicate with your partner?

_____

_____

Congratulations on completing these questions. You undoubtedly have a unique and fresh perspective on life in your partner's skin after doing this exercise. Now take a few minutes to review your experience with your spouse. Compare notes and invite feedback about your take on life as your partner.

Chapter 10

LOVE LIFE

Love must be learned, and learned again and again; there is no end to it.

—KATHERINE ANNE PORTER

When asked "What makes a good marriage?" the answer given by nearly 90 percent of the population is "Being in love."[1] When respondents were asked to list the essential ingredients of love as a basis for marriage, however, a survey of more than a thousand college students revealed that "no single item was mentioned by at least one half of those responding." In other words, we can't agree on what love is. Or perhaps more accurately, we don't *know* what love is. As one survey respondent said, "Love is like lightning—you may not know what it is, but you do know when it hits you."

In *Twelfth Night.* Shakespeare asked: "What is love?" The question has echoed for centuries, and still there is no definitive answer. Is love the *self-seeking* desire described by William Blake's poem: "Love seeketh only self to please"? Or is love the *self-sacrificial* stance described by the apostle Paul: "Love bears all things, believes all things, hopes all things, endures all things"?

Whatever love is, it is not easy to pin down, because love is a strange mixture of opposites. It includes affection and anger, excitement and boredom, stability and

81

change, restriction and freedom. Love's ultimate paradox is two beings becoming one, yet remaining two.

HOW YOU VIEW LOVE IN PRACTICAL TERMS

Theories and philosophies have their place, but it's time to get practical. If you look up the word *practical* in the dictionary it will tell you that it means "sensible" and "usable." And that's exactly what we want this section of this chapter to be for you. We want you to come away from this section with better understanding but also actual things you can do to love each other more and better.

How I Like to Be Loved

The top of this page of your SYMBIS+ Report provides a little snapshot of the practical expression of love in marriage—based on your personality. Take a moment to read them aloud to each other, then mark where you fall on the following continuum.

This accurately sums up my view of love with you.

NOT ACCURATE AT ALL   VERY ACCURATE

| 1 | 2 | 3 | 4 | 5 | 6 | 7 | 8 | 9 | 10 |

Why? _____

_____

_____

Seeing my spouse's view of love in practical terms makes me feel that I can better love my spouse by [be specific and use an example]:

_____

_____

_____

If I were to give one real-life example to my spouse on how to better express love to me in practical terms, this is what comes to mind (use a concrete example):

_____

_____

_____

In hearing an example from your spouse of how you might better express love in practical terms, what do you think?

NEVER GOING TO HAPPEN   I CAN DO THAT!

1	2	3	4	5	6	7	8	9	10

Why? _____

_____

_____

How would you expound on your view of love in practical terms? In other words, what else is important to you when it comes to summing up love in practical terms specifically for you?

HOW EACH OF YOU WOULD IMPROVE YOUR SEX LIFE

The movie *Old School,* starring Will Ferrell as Frank "the Tank," captures the erroneous belief that marriage eventually kills your sex life. Vince Vaughn's character mocks one of his recently married buddies for deciding to have sex with only one person for the rest of his life.

But the real joke, for those in the know, is on him. Why? Marriage actually makes sex better.

The fantasy of single people out on the town every night having wild sex is just that—a fantasy. In fact, according to the landmark "Sex in America" survey, published in the *New England Journal of Medicine*, the people having the most sex are monogamous married couples.[2] And that's not all: married sex is more fun. In a news report about the sex lives of married couples, ABC's John Stossel interviewed Mark and Dawna Nocera, award-winning professional dancers who teach at their studio in Woburn, Massachusetts. After fifteen years of marriage, they say their sex life has never been hotter. They say a great marriage and great sex is very much like a dance. "Somebody who's just starting out dancing doesn't know anything about the experience that you have twenty years later when you really move," said Mark Nocera. "I think sex is very much like that. It takes a lot of rehearsal to make dancing look that easy."[3]

 If you were to liken your sex life to dancing, who typically takes the lead? Do you both like it that way? Why or why not?

The British health magazine *Top Sante* commissioned a National Sex and Relationship Survey and found that sex for married women is just as good as it is for men. Among the findings was that after fourteen years of marriage, 63 percent of women still fancy their husband "just as much as when they first met him."

> There are as many minds as there are heads, so there are as many kinds of love as there are hearts.
> —Leo Tolstoy

Juliette Kellow, editor of *Top Sante*, comments, "This survey turns on its head the idea that the best sex is when we are footloose, fancy free, and single. The truth is, truly great sex and deep intimacy are most likely to happen within the trusting, committed environment of marriage."

Juliette is right. But this isn't what we hear—or see depicted in film or on TV. Married couples are the designated losers in our hormone-obsessed culture. The late-night comics, for example, would have you believe that the sex lives of married couples are in danger of dwindling into either mechanical routine or total extinction. And a University of Chicago study found that married couples in the movies are rarely depicted as having a great sex life.[4]

Do you ever feel like everyone else seems to have a better sex life than the two of you? Why or why not?

The people most apt to report that they are very satisfied with their current sex life are married couples who believe sex outside of marriage is wrong.[5] In fact, "traditionalists" rank an astounding 31 percentage points higher in their level of sexual satisfaction than singles who have no objection to sex outside of marriage. The findings contribute to a growing body of research linking sexual satisfaction to marital harmony, fidelity and permanence.[6]

You might be saying that's all well and good, but when it comes to sex in our marriage there's plenty of room for improvement. We get that. Join the club. The ideal of full-throttle and lifelong passion in marriage is unreasonable—especially for couples juggling time constraints, career pressures, parenting schedules, family commitments, and all the rest. Every married couple needs help in this area on occasion. That's why it important to honestly answer the question: How would you improve your sex life?

Improving Our Sex Life

To help you begin an honest discussion about how you can mutually improve your sex life, try completing these sentence stems and then discuss them with each other.

My spouse's answer to this question is . . .

_____

_____

In considering my spouse's answer, I think . . .

_____

_____

In considering my spouse's answer, I feel . . .

_____

_____

_____

LET'S TALK ABOUT SEX

Very often a husband and wife can be married for many years without ever telling each other what they find most exciting in bed. This is partly because many people remain painfully embarrassed about their sexual needs. But it's also because too much is at stake—namely, the emotional bond between husbands and wives. To gamble it on fulfilling a need that might be seen as odd, selfish, or simply beyond the comfort level of their partner is too risky. And after years pass, it often becomes more and more difficult to reveal a "hidden" desire, because it feels like introducing something very foreign into the relationship, not to mention that it's like admitting that you've been fibbing about your sexual desires all that time. But we can assure you that this talk is worth the risk as long as you approach it carefully.

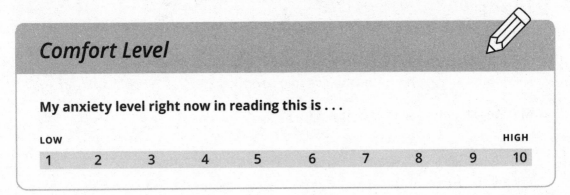

Comfort Level

My anxiety level right now in reading this is . . .

LOW									HIGH
1	2	3	4	5	6	7	8	9	10

HOW DO YOU RATE YOUR DESIRE?

You can see how each of you rate your personal desire for sex on your report. Are they about the same? If so, great! But chances are they differ a little or a lot from time to time.

Of course, in a perfect world, the two of you would have flawlessly matched libidos all the time—but we know that's never going to be the case. You can't expect your spouse's sex drive to always match your own. But there's hope for getting better aligned if one of you is hearing the "headache" excuse a little more frequently than you should be.

After all, perpetual libido differences can drive a wedge between a husband and wife. So for the sake of your marriage, as well as your sex life, it's essential to keep those differences to a minimum.

Find What You're Looking For

We're going to dedicate this exercise primarily to the husband. Why? Because there is ample evidence that men typically rate their desire higher than their wives do. Of course, that's not always true and you can reverse the scenario if that's the case in your marriage. So here we go.

First, it's true that you find what you're looking for. If you want evidence to indicate that your wife doesn't want sex as much as you do, you'll find plenty of it. But if you're ready to equal the scales of sexual desire, you need to get over this common male myth by seeing her in a new light.

If I'm honest, I sometimes look for and find evidence that my spouse doesn't want to have sex with me. I may even make snide comments about it.

TRUE									FALSE
1	2	3	4	5	6	7	8	9	10

One of the best ways to end snide comments or innuendos is to realize that you are highlighting a perceived libido difference. Every time you say something, even under your breath, like, "Well, if we ever had sex . . . ," you're driving a sexual wedge between you. By the way, this means not only forgoing these comments not only with her but when you're out with the boys as well. Set your mind to seeing your wife on the same side as you. She wants to have a great sex life as much as you do. And if you don't believe us, just ask her.

I'm willing to pledge right now that I will work to refrain from making snide comments and trying to build a case against my spouse for not having the same sex drive.

NO I WON'T   YES I WILL

| 1 | 2 | 3 | 4 | 5 | 6 | 7 | 8 | 9 | 10 |

Talking about your sex drives is not a common conversation for most couples. Yet it's critically important for getting your libidos to line up.

 When the time is right, when both of you are relatively relaxed and not distracted, ask each other: When do you feel friskiest?

I (Les) have a friend who told me he recently discovered that his wife found him sexiest when he wore a suit. He joked about wearing it to bed. The point is that you need to know as much as you can about each other's sexual desires. Ask about the time of day. And for her, ask about the time of month she is most inclined to want to have sex. Ask each other what would make it easier or more fun, too.

ARE YOU COMFORTABLE TALKING ABOUT SEX?

You can see how each of you addressed your personal comfort level right there on your report. If you both feel totally relaxed and comfortable having an honest conversation about your sex life as a couple, count yourselves blessed. You are in a small minority and you can probably skip the rest of this section. If not, we have a helpful exercise for you.

Let's Talk about Sex, Baby

If you're feeling even a little nervous about discussing your sex life with each other in a truly open and honest way, begin by putting yourself in each other's shoes. Mutual empathy goes a long way here.

When it comes to talking about sex in our marriage, my spouse is probably feeling . . .

_____

_____

_____

The reason I'm a bit nervous about discussing sex with my spouse is . . .

_____

_____

_____

Now that you've taken a moment to help each other empathize, it's time to talk. Really talk about what you would like from your sex life together. Don't be shy about telling what you like and what you don't like. But be gentle here—you want to make things better, not cause hurt feelings. Also, discuss what you would like to try.

WHAT YOU LIKE	WHAT YOU DON'T LIKE	WHAT YOU'D LIKE TO TRY

As you review your lists together, ask questions. Be open to hearing what your spouse has to say. Encourage openness by listening well to each other. If something is brought up that one of you is uncomfortable with, respect that and move on to the next thing. Never try to force your spouse to try something they are uncomfortable doing or make them feel guilty about their feelings and preferences.

By the way, if talking about your sex life is too embarrassing or uncomfortable for either one of you, write out your thoughts and questions for each other. This method will take a little longer but will accomplish the same goal.

WHO DO YOU EXPECT TO INITIATE SEX?

In most couples, one spouse typically doesn't like to be the one who initiates sex. They are simply uncomfortable saying something like, "Would you like to make love?"

Don't make the mistake of attributing a hesitancy to initiate to a lack of libido. Instead, make it easier for both of you to initiate sex. How? Find a sign or a signal to make initiation almost effortless. For example, maybe one of you could light a special candle or play a particular song, or maybe you could just give each other a certain look.

 What would make initiating sex easier for you? More specifically, what signal could the two of you have that would indicate you'd like to have sex?

HOW OFTEN DO YOU EXPECT TO HAVE SEX?

Chances are that if you've been married for a few years, your expectations for the frequency of sex in your relationship may not match up. Often the man wants sex more frequently than the woman. Is that what is indicated in your individual answers to this question? If so, make no mistake, a woman's libido (and thus her frequency meter for sex) is more complicated than a man's libido.

WHY FREQUENCY IS MORE COMPLICATED FOR WOMEN

How is it that a husband and wife can view the frequency of sex so differently? The answer is found, in great part, in understanding how a woman becomes sexually aroused and motivated. Too often, men assume that the way a woman's libido works is (or should be) the same way a man's libido works. But it's not that simple. In fact, understanding a woman's sex drive requires a bit of study. "Every woman is a science," said John Donne. And if you take a moment to study your wife, you will discover that her libido, though quite different than yours, is more powerful than you think.

Here are some of the most important points in understanding the female libido.

1. WOMEN EQUATE SEX WITH EMOTIONAL ASSURANCE

One reason for the perceived distinction in male-female motivations for sex is that we are socialized in different ways about sexuality and marriage. Men tend to see sex as a pleasurable, physical activity. Not necessarily so for women. Most women see sex as a sign of emotional bonding with their husband. She needs to feel sure of your emotional togetherness before she wants to express physical togetherness. (Keep in mind that the items in this section are for the woman to answer.)

Do You Feel What I Feel?

Relative to your husband, do you see sex more as emotional bonding than physical pleasure?

NOT TRUE FOR ME | | | | | | | | | VERY TRUE FOR ME

| 1 | 2 | 3 | 4 | 5 | 6 | 7 | 8 | 9 | 10 |

Why?_____

_____

_____

---

2. WOMEN WITHHOLD SEX WHEN FEELING HURT

Let's say your wife spoke harshly to you because you left your dirty socks on the floor. You think she overreacted. You're perturbed. Maybe even angry. A few minutes pass and she walks into your den wearing nothing but a string of pearls around her neck and high heeled shoes. Now tell me, are you going to punish her by withholding sex because she hollered at you just minutes earlier about your dirty socks?

I don't even need to hear your answer.

But you probably need to hear your wife's answer when the roles are reversed. Why? Because unresolved emotional issues, even little ones, are often at the root of low libidos for women. Resentment, unexpressed anger, and hurt feelings can lead some women to withhold sex. Maybe she's too upset with you to let you touch her.

Say, for example, she feels taken for granted because you don't help around the house as much as she'd like. She thinks "If he isn't doing something for me, why should I have sex with him?" Now, of course you'd probably never dream of depriving yourself of sex in order to punish your wife, but women are wired differently. She can put her libido on hold until she regains the "emotional assurance" that tells her you're on her team. (Again, keep in mind that these items in this section are for the woman to answer.)

Hold On

As a woman, do you agree with the above sentiment about withholding sex when your feelings get hurt?

NOT TRUE FOR ME   VERY TRUE FOR ME

| 1 | 2 | 3 | 4 | 5 | 6 | 7 | 8 | 9 | 10 |

Why? _____

_____

_____

3. WOMEN ARE MORE "HORMONAL" THAN MEN

If you're hearing "I'm not in the mood" when you want to hear "come hither" whispers from your wife, it may be because her mood is being determined by her hormones. Her disinterest likely has nothing to do with your sexual attractiveness. Biological changes are far more likely to sap her libido than they are to sap yours. When was the last time you weren't "in the mood"? Is your memory failing you on this one? That's because, if you're like most men, you can generally get in the mood at the drop of a hat (or any other article of clothing). You're typically not battling a surge of hormones that causes you to question your body image or your wife's acceptance of you.

And, let's be honest, men don't have to deal with "that time of the month," and all the hormonal mood swings that can come with it. Not to mention the physical cramping. When she turns you down because she's "too tired," it's most likely true.

Here's the point: For a woman, hormones can mean she feels like having lots of sex at a particular time rather than sex all of the time.

And to avoid the questions we're likely to get on our website, let us tell you exactly when that "particular time" is. It has to do with a neurochemical called oxytocin, often referred to as the bonding hormone. It spikes right before ovulation, a time when most women are in the mood. And here's some really good news: oxytocin also helps dull your wife's memory of your annoying traits (like your dirty socks on the floor). In other words, this is also when she is likely to feel most attracted to you.

In the Mood

As a woman, do you agree that, relative to your husband, your libido (because of hormonal cycles) can be a bit of a roller coaster?

NOT TRUE FOR ME | | | | | | | | VERY TRUE FOR ME

| 1 | 2 | 3 | 4 | 5 | 6 | 7 | 8 | 9 | 10 |

Why?_____

_____

4. A WOMAN'S SEX DRIVE CAN BE MORE EASILY DISTRACTED

Okay. So you've given your wife "the look." It says, "Let's go!" You're ready to rumble. She gets the message but says, "I'll come to bed right after I fold this laundry" . . . or "make the kids' lunch for tomorrow" . . . or "take out the recycling." As a man, you can't imagine doing any of those things yourself if your wife were to give you "the look." You're ready to go. Now. So why isn't she?

The reason is that men are often able to get aroused and sexually ready more quickly than women. This is critically important to understand. We're not only talking about foreplay once you and your wife are between the sheets. That's a given. We're talking about even just being ready to enter the bedroom with sex on your mind.

Women don't want anything distracting them from sex once their sexual engine is about to be turned on. That's why they take more care than a man does to go through their mental checklist. They need to be sure the kids are in bed, the door is locked, the shades are shut, and so on. They don't want any loose ends keeping them from focusing on sex once you get started.

It's a fact. Your wife is far more vulnerable to distraction from sex than you are, and that can keep her sexual engine from starting when you want it to. But don't discount her sex drive because of it. It's just different than yours. If she has an unfinished task, let her finish it. Better yet, help her finish it. You'll be amazed how her libido picks up steam, and you'll be pleased to see how fully present she is while you're making love. An undistracted woman, given time to rev up her sexual engine, will be far more "into it" than a woman who feels pressured and duty-bound to be ready to go at a moment's notice.

Getting Into It

Relative to your husband, do you feel that unfinished business and tasks can distract you from getting in the mood?

NOT TRUE FOR ME   VERY TRUE FOR ME

| 1 | 2 | 3 | 4 | 5 | 6 | 7 | 8 | 9 | 10 |

Why?_____

_____

_____

 What is the most practical insight you each gained from this section on sex and how will it make a difference in your relationship?

Chapter 11

ATTITUDE

We were promised sufferings. They were part of the program.
We were even told, "Blessed are they that mourn," and I
accept it. I've got nothing that I hadn't bargained for.

—C. S. LEWIS

We had just finished speaking at a retreat in the San Juan Islands when a plane that was to take us to another engagement buzzed overhead and landed on a nearby airstrip. Five minutes later we boarded the three-person, rickety-looking Cessna.

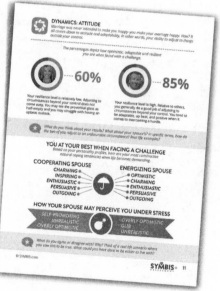

The pilot greeted us. "It's gonna be a little noisy up there," he said, "but it's a short hop back to Seattle and a real beauty this time of the evening."

We looked at each other, silently communicating our mutual fear about traveling in such a tiny aircraft. "Great!" Leslie managed to reply.

We secured our belts and headphones as the pilot started the engine. In no time at all we were barreling down the grass runway, three deer scattering into the woods before us. Forgetting our fear, we leaned close to the windows, watching a small rim of sunlight glisten off the snowy peaks of the Cascade Mountains. The sight was truly glorious.

We crossed over the islands of Puget Sound and approached the lights of a local airport. "The most important thing about landing is the attitude of the plane," said the pilot.

"You mean altitude, don't you?" I asked.

"No. The attitude has to do with the nose of the plane," the pilot explained. "If the attitude is too high, the plane will come down with a severe bounce. And if the attitude is too low, the plane may go out of control because of excessive landing speed."

Then the pilot said something that got our attention: *"The trick is to get the right attitude in spite of atmospheric conditions."*

Without knowing it, our pilot had given us a perfect metaphor for creating a happy marriage—the trick is to develop the right attitude in spite of the circumstances we find ourselves in.

It is no accident that some *couples* who encounter marital turbulence navigate it successfully, while others in similar circumstances are buffeted by frustration, disappointment, and eventual despair. It is also no accident that some *couples* are positive and happy, while other *couples* are beaten down and defeated. Researchers who have investigated the difference between the two groups have come up with all kinds of explanations for marital success (long courtships, similar backgrounds, supportive families, good communication, good educations, and so on). But the bottom line is that happy *couples decide* to be happy. In spite of the troubles life deals them, they make happiness a choice.

As a couple, we have taught university courses on marriage for two decades, and we have at least two dozen of the latest academic textbooks on marriage and family in our personal library. One of our favorite textbooks, considered a classic by many, has in it an italicized sentence that bears repeating: *"The most important characteristic of a marriageable person is the habit of happiness."*[1] Why? Because happiness in marriage has nothing to do with luck and everything to do with will. In other words, happiness comes down to having the right attitude in spite of atmospheric conditions.

When confronted with a difficult situation, a person with an outstanding attitude makes the best of it while he gets the worst of it.
—John C. Maxwell

Atmospheric Conditions

Imagine for a moment that both of you are meteorologists. You're experts at understanding what defines the weather: the various combinations of temperature, wind, barometric pressure, humidity, clouds, and precipitation. You understand weather patterns that determine the quality of the atmosphere.

Draw a quick picture of the current weather conditions of your marriage. Don't worry about your artistic skills. That's not the point. Simply depict the current climate in your relationship and be as creative as you like.

Share your drawings with each other and describe what's going on—what various things represent. Be sure to be non-defensive. Seek to understand and be understanding. Be gentle with each other.

If you were to describe the qualities that predict a proverbial sunny day—an ideal day in your marriage—what would be a part of it? Describe up to a half dozen things that come to mind, and be specific. For example, you might say that you'd both have a good night's sleep and wake up rested together. You get the idea. Go for it:

_____

_____

_____

Review your list and note what is likely to interfere with your sunny forecast. What conditions could potentially mess up the ideal conditions? What would represent ominous clouds, high winds, or excessive precipitation in your marriage? For example, maybe it's misunderstandings about your schedules. Or a discrepancy in how to discipline a child. Come up with a half dozen things that seem to interfere with happiness in your marriage:

_____

_____

_____

What are some of the *severe* weather conditions you've experienced at some point in your marriage? What are the proverbial thunderstorms (or maybe even ice storms, dust storms, cyclones, or tornadoes) you've encountered?

_____

_____

_____

Okay. You can take off your "meteorologist" hat and think about the exercise you've just completed. What are you learning from each other? If you're like most couples, when you review the things that interfere with your happiness and when you recall the big jolts you've encountered as a couple, you'll see that all of them could be improved by your attitude.

Do you agree that your attitude can go a long way in improving the "atmospheric conditions" of your relationship? Why or why not?

YOUR PERCENTILE

At the top of this page of your SYMBIS+ Report you will find a percentage. Yikes! These can be scary for some of us because we can't help but to see them as a score, a rank, or a grade. Your mind might go to thinking of a credit score, an SAT ranking, or a bodyfat percentile. But don't worry. That's not the case here. As your SYMBIS Facilitator has probably already explained, the number at the top of this page simply represents your current self-assessment of how optimistic, adaptable, and resilient you are feeling—particularly when you are faced with a challenge.

Consider this number as simply a current barometer reading. As you probably know, a barometer is an instrument used to forecast the weather. A needle moves to various places on a dial to show how conditions are changing. And one thing you can count on—the needle *will* change.

The same is true for your current number. It's simply showing you how optimistic, adaptable, and resilient you are currently feeling. So don't get hung up on this being a "score" that defines you. It isn't, and it doesn't.

 How do you feel about your current percentage? Is it generally accurate? Explain what's going on behind your feelings.

Let's break down the elements of what goes into your percentile on this page by looking at optimism, adaptability, and resiliency. The following exercises will help you do just that.

OPTIMISM

Few traits are more strongly linked to personal happiness than seeing the glass as half full as opposed to half empty. Hundreds if not thousands of studies show that optimism leads to better consequences than pessimism.[2] Optimistic people have been shown to achieve more, build stronger relationships, and have better health. Optimists are also superior at deflecting depression and bouncing back from hardship. Optimists believe what Victor Hugo wrote in Les Miserables: "Even the darkest night will end and the sun will rise."

Does being optimistic mean we are blind to reality? Absolutely not. The recipe for abiding happiness includes ample optimism to provide hope, a dash of pessimism to prevent complacency, and enough realism to distinguish those things we can control from those we cannot. It's what theologian Reinhold Niebuhr offered in his "Serenity Prayer": "O God, give us grace to accept with serenity the things that cannot be changed, courage to change the things which should be changed, and the wisdom to distinguish the one from the other."

Half Full or Half Empty?

I'm an optimistic person (and most people would see me as such).

NOT TRUE FOR ME									VERY TRUE FOR ME
1	2	3	4	5	6	7	8	9	10

Why? _____

_____

I'm a pessimistic person (and most people would see me as such).

NOT TRUE FOR ME									VERY TRUE FOR ME
1	2	3	4	5	6	7	8	9	10

Why? _____

_____

I'm a realistic person (and most people would see me as such).

NOT TRUE FOR ME   VERY TRUE FOR ME

| 1 | 2 | 3 | 4 | 5 | 6 | 7 | 8 | 9 | 10 |

Why? _____

_____

 What is your biggest self-insight after completing this exercise on optimism and how does it compare to your partner's?

ADAPTABILITY

The second factor that goes into an attitude that has learned to adjust to things beyond its control is adaptability. When the weather is miserable, an adaptable attitude doesn't get worked up and whine about it. It adjusts to the new conditions. It makes the best of the situation.

If you struggle with this capability, like most people do, consider your personal "agendas." This is a proven means to help you become more adaptable. What are your personal agendas? You might have an agenda about what's taking place for dinner. You might have an agenda about how the dishes should go into the dishwasher. You might have an agenda about what kind of vacation you take. We all have agendas all the time. You have an agenda about what you will do when you complete this exercise.

The question becomes how flexible you are with your agendas. Why? Because flexibility determines your adaptability. The less flexible you are with your own agendas, the more self-focused or egocentric you tend to be.

When you can set aside your personal agenda—just temporarily—and be open to another one, you become flexible. You adjust to the stormy weather and control your attitude rather than letting the weather control you.

How Adaptable Are You?

This little self-test will require you to be brutally honest with yourself. It will give you a glimpse into your self-focus and thus how flexible you are with your personal agendas.

In the center section of the table below, mark one of the center columns, labeled 1 through 5, to indicate which side of that row best matches how you feel. If you strongly agree with the right side, mark the 5 box, putting a 5 in it. If you don't know, mark the 3, putting a 3 in it. If you strongly agree with the left side, mark the 1 box putting a 1 in it.

Again, be honest with yourself as you choose between the sets of statements.

LEFT SIDE	1	2	3	4	5	RIGHT SIDE
I often doubt my view of things.						My view of things is always correct.
I don't mind being wrong.						I hate being wrong.
I look for valid criticisms so I can improve.						Criticisms of me are not true.
I know I can usually correct my mistakes.						It is very important to never make a mistake.
If you contradict me, I look to see if you are correct.						If you contradict me, you are obviously wrong.
If you make a good argument I can easily change my view.						I automatically defend my viewpoint, no matter what the other person says.
It doesn't bother me to lose an argument.						If I lose an argument, I feel bad inside.
I look for the value in other people's arguments.						Other people's arguments are worthless.
The real truth is more important than my view.						My view is the real truth.
Subtotal scores ➜						Add across this row for your total score: _____

Scoring: Add up all the numbers in the five columns. Then add the subtotals in the last row (across the five columns) to achieve your total score. It should fall within the range of 9 to 45. If your answers are accurate, here's what your score means:

9 to 19—Your score indicates that you have relatively few egocentric tendencies in your disposition. In other words, relative to other people, you are less inclined to be focused on yourself. This bodes well for your capacity to set aside your own agenda with your spouse. You already tend to do this quite instinctively. If your score is on the especially low end of this range, however, you may need to give special attention to making sure you express your own needs more forthrightly. You may need to exert more assertiveness. You can do this by simply finishing this sentence more often: "If it were up to me, I would . . ." This technique allows you to be more up front about your own needs while still maintaining a healthy other-focused perspective.

If you struggle with this capability, like most people do, consider your personal "agendas." This is a proven means to help you become more adaptable. What are your personal agendas? You might have an agenda about what's taking place for dinner. You might have an agenda about how the dishes should go into the dishwasher. You might have an agenda about what kind of vacation you take. We all have agendas all the time. You have an agenda about what you will do when you complete this exercise.

20 to 35—Your score is in the midrange of egocentric tendencies. Sometimes you are inclined to set aside your own needs brilliantly, but other times you struggle to do so. In fact, the times when you struggle may be quite predictable. For many people who score in this range, the selfish tendencies tend to appear most when they are feeling hungry, stressed, or tired. Is this the case for you? If so, sometimes the simple acknowledgment of this fact can be enough to help you remedy the situation. You can say something like, "I'm having a tough time focusing on anyone other than myself at the moment because . . ." This assertion will help you and your spouse recognize that it's not the most opportune time for you to set aside your own needs.

36 to 45—Your score indicates an intense level of egocentric tendencies. You have a tough time setting aside your own agenda because of a fear that your own needs may not get met. As a result, you will need to give special attention to setting your own needs on the back burner. At times this may be a deep struggle for you, but with a little practice you can make significant improvements. Begin by acknowledging that your egocentric tendencies are real. You may not want to face this fact, but once you do you will have taken a big step in changing this self-centered focus. Second, realize that this is only temporary. You're not required to "trade places" with your spouse without getting your needs met. In fact, just the opposite is true. Once you enjoy mutual empathy your needs will get met like never before. Third, complete this sentence when you are ready to set aside your own needs: "If I were my spouse, I would feel or think . . ." You can also complete this sentence to yourself: "My spouse has a valid point because . . ." Or try this exercise: If you're in an irritable mood and projecting negative energy toward your spouse, visualize for a moment that your spouse is you. Do you appreciate the way you are being treated? That's the key question for you, and it will help you transcend your own ego.

Once you have reviewed the meaning of your personal score on this self-test, compare with your spouse and talk about where the two of you tend to fall on the following continuum. Place your names at the appropriate places:

9	25	45

- How do your scores compare? Do you both agree with where you landed? Why or why not?

- Which one of you may have the tougher time setting aside your own agenda? How can you help each other do this better?

- Are there predictable times when you think your self-centered ways are most likely to interfere with your attempts to trade places? What are they?

Before we leave the exercise, we want to give you a practical tool for when the two of you are struggling with a specific issue that may be difficult for both of you to see from the same perspective. Do you have an issue like that in mind? To use this method you will need something specific in mind. Here's what to do:

First, on a sheet of paper, write out all of your beliefs about why your perspective is right (this is the easy part!).

Next, switch sides. Put aside your own beliefs for a moment and write down all the reasons you can think of that indicate your spouse's perspective (their beliefs and feelings) is right and you are wrong.

Now reflect on both sides and consider the truth in both perspectives. Discuss any new perspectives you have gained.

RESILIENCY

Every marriage, no matter how good it is, eventually bumps into something bad. Guaranteed. We often tell newlyweds to put on your seatbelt. Eventually you're going to hit a jolt you didn't see coming. It's inevitable. And one of the saving graces of your relationship during these tough times will be your capacity to adjust—to be resilient.

Resilience is the ability to mentally and emotionally cope with a crisis. It's the ability to use our psychological and spiritual capabilities to remain relatively calm during chaos and to move on from it with minimal long-term negative consequences. What is your personal capacity to demonstrate resiliency?

How Resilient Are You?

Earlier in this chapter you noted a few proverbial thunderstorms that you've encountered. These are big jolts to your life and your relationship. They might have to do with a financial problem, a health crisis, or maybe a relationship failure.

Review the list you made earlier. Feel free to add to it if you like. Once you have these times in mind, consider how you responded to them. List some of the things you did to keep your chin up and what you may have done that didn't work so well.

POSITIVE WAYS I COPED	NEGATIVE WAYS I COPED

 What is your biggest self-insight after completing this exercise on resiliency, and how does it compare to your partner's?

Chapter 12

COMMUNICATION

It is terrible to speak well and be wrong.

—Sophocles

"So how was your day?" you ask your husband.

"Good. It was good."

"What happened?"

"Same old stuff, really. Nothing new."

"Isn't it great to finally have some time to ourselves?" you say, undaunted by the false start to what is certain to be a meaningful heart-to-heart conversation.

"Yeah," he says as he looks around the restaurant.

"You seem distracted."

"No. Not at all. I just wondered if the game was over and who won."

"Okay," you say slowly, raising the pitch of your voice as you drag out the word.

He picks up on the message and attempts to turn things around. "It doesn't really matter who won the game. Let's talk."

That's when you look at each other blankly and wonder what you have to talk about. A plethora of words is primed and ready for a great exchange somewhere within your vocal cords, yet nothing comes out. So you sip your coffee, and wrack your brain for the start of a meaningful conversation.

If you didn't already know, let's put it on the table: The number one problem couples report is "a breakdown in communication." And with good reason. Whether a relationship sinks or swims depends on how well partners send and receive messages, how well they use their conversations to understand and be understood. Think about it. If you are feeling especially close to your partner, it is because you are communicating well. Your spirits are up. Your love life is full. You are in tune. But when communication falls flat, when you feel stuck and you're talking in circles, relational satisfaction drops. Communication, more than any other aspect of your relationship, can either buoy relational intimacy or be the dead weight of its demise.

That's why we are so excited for you to drill down into the personalized content on the communication page of your SYMBIS+ Report. Before you do, however, we want to have you start off by assessing your overall communication smarts.

Communication Basics

The following questions will give you a general idea of how you are doing when it comes to the basics of communication. Each of you should answer these simple questions as honestly as you can.

T	F	What I say is more important than how I say it.
T	F	When we are in sync, my partner should almost be able to read my mind.
T	F	The basic goal of good communication in a loving relationship is to convey information accurately.
T	F	The children's rhyme is right: "Words can never hurt you."
T	F	If you're not talking, you're not communicating.
T	F	The best communicators accurately get their point across first, then they try to understand their partner.
T	F	Using "I" statements (rather than "you" statements) is self-centered.

T **F** Good relational communication between partners always involves logical thinking.

T **F** Physical touch is a low-level priority in effective communication between partners.

T **F** Communication differences between men and women are relatively minor.

_____ Total True Answers

_____ Total False Answers

If you have eight or more false answers, congratulations. You are well on your way to having the basics of good talk under your belt, and you are primed to benefit significantly from this page of your SYMBIS+ Report. If your score isn't as high, don't feel bad. You're not alone and you will probably benefit from a quick brush-up on the fundamentals outlined in our book *Love Talk*. There you will find an easy-to-read overview of the most important skills required for good communication.

By the way, even if you answered "false" to all ten of these questions, you're not necessarily immune to conversations that fall flat. This is just the starting place to give you a sense of where you stand when it comes to the basics. One more thing. This exercise is not about scoring better than your partner. It's not a competition. So if you did better than your partner on this exercise, take the higher ground and don't make a big deal out of it. Have some fun with your scores if your partner is in a playful mood, but don't press your luck.

 What do you make of how you each came out on this true/false exercise? Do you need to brush up on the basics of good communication? Why or why not?

Early on in our marriage we seemed to talk about everything. Nothing was off limits. We talked at length about our dreams, our struggles, our fears, and our triumphs. In short, we were vulnerable. We shared things we didn't dare share with anyone else. But somewhere along the line (certainly after our children were born), these heart-to-heart chitchats dwindled . . .along with the intimacy they engendered. We were still talking, of course, but we weren't having the kind of vulnerable talks we once shared.

"You can have a two-hour conversation and not talk about anything of substance or value or quality," says Terri Orbuch at the Institute for Social Research at the University of Michigan. She and her colleagues studied 373 married couples for more than twenty years and came up with a prescription for increasing emotional intimacy: ten minutes a day of quality conversation. That's it.

"Many couples think they're communicating with each other when they sort out who will pick up the kids, pay the bills, or call the grandparents," says Orbuch. But that's not the kind of communication she's talking about. Her research and that of many others consistently shows a link between happy marriages and "self-disclosure," or the sharing of your private feelings, fears, doubts, and perceptions with your partner.

> A kiss is a lovely trick designed by nature to stop speech when words become superfluous.
>
> —Ingrid Bergman

Why is this important? The early stages of marriage, research shows, are characterized by open and frequent conversations, but such behavior typically declines if couples are not intentional—especially when kids come along. In other words, as your marriage matures, self-disclosure risks leveling off.[1] Don't let that happen. Too much is at stake. Try Dr. Orbuch's advice. We did. Rarely does a day go by that we don't have at least ten minutes of vulnerable talk time. It typically occurs after our boys are tucked in and the house is quiet. Occasionally it happens over lunch together, depending on our schedules. What do we talk about? We focus on the 5 percent of our life we generally don't discuss with others. Of course, to reclaim the heart-to-heart connections you may be missing, you have to find the time to do so.

Finding Time to Talk

Someone once said that the one thing you can't recycle is wasted time. How true. But you can often find more time for what matters most—if you are willing to look for it. Accurately assessing how you spend your time in an average week is the key to finding more time. Each week is made up of 168 hours. How does it divvy up for you? Completing the following items will show you.

Number of hours you sleep each night _____ × 7 = _____

Number of hours you work (or attend school) each week _____

Number of hours per day spent on food preparation and eating _____ × 7 = _____

Number of hours per day spent on grooming _____ × 7 = _____

Number of hours per day spent on exercise _____ × 7 = _____

Number of hours per day spent on commuting _____ × 7 = _____

Number of hours per day spent on socializing with friends _____ × 7 = _____

Number of hours per day spent on entertainment (TV, video games, web surfing, reading, hobby, etc.) _____ × 7 = _____

Number of hours per day spent on email and phone outside of work _____ × 7 = _____

Now add up the totals: _____

Subtract the above number from 168: 168–_____ = _____

These are the remaining hours you have for one-on-one time with your partner.

Now that you've identified how you are spending most of your time, consider these questions as a starter for helping you create more time together:

Does the amount of potential time you have for talking with your partner surprise you? Why or why not?

_____

_____

_____

If you are wanting to find more time together, what can you do? What aspects of your schedule can realistically be changed to permit more time for the two of you?

_____

_____

_____

Even if you have time together, it may not be "quality" time. What do you think? Is it? Why or why not? If not, what can you do to increase the quality of the time you have together?

_____

_____

_____

The 80–20 Rule, originally set forth by Italian economist Vilfredo Pareto, states that 80 percent of the reward comes from 20 percent of the effort. How would you identify the valuable 20 percent that brings you and your partner closer together?

_____

_____

_____

**Have you talked about your biological prime time? That's the time of day
you are at your best. Knowing when your best time is can help you optimize
your one-on-one time together. Are you a morning person, a night owl, or
a late-afternoon whiz? If you are out of sync with each other's biological
prime time, what can you do to compensate for that?**

_____

_____

_____

YOUR TALK STYLE

At the top of this page of your SYMBIS+ Report is a paragraph that describes how you
are hardwired for conversations. Don't get too caught up in how accurate it is. You can
certainly disagree with anything you read here. In fact, if you haven't already done so
with your SYMBIS Facilitator, scratch out any statement you don't think is true of you.
But before you do so, talk about it. Explain why you disagree with it and see if your
spouse agrees.

After reviewing these personalized paragraphs with each other, talk about
what you got out of each one. What is your main take-away about yourself?
What is the main thing you discovered regarding your spouse?

HOW DO YOU LIKE YOUR SPOUSE TO COMMUNICATE WITH YOU?

Review this portion of the SYMBIS+ Report. If you haven't done so already, select the two items (of the five) that you resonate with most and explain why they are important to you. Use specific examples so that your spouse can see more clearly when and how to do this for you.

What is one specific example of how you plan to communicate in a way that your partner will appreciate? Ask your spouse if you're headed in the right direction for improving how the two of you communicate.

As you consider the ways each of you can tailor your communication to better suit each other, we can tell you that you'll both benefit from "listening with the third ear." That's what psychologist Theodor Reich called it. We're referring to the capacity every husband and wife have to listen not just to the words their partner is saying but to the emotions underlying them. And not only to listen, but to reflect back those feelings to see if they have been accurately understood or not. This seemingly simple skill is one of the most valuable tools we've ever found for helping to open up each other's spirit for a truly meaningful conversation.

Listening with Your Third Ear

It's not so much what your partner is saying to you—it's what you *hear* your partner saying to you. That's why reflecting your spouse's feelings is one of the most helpful yet difficult listening techniques to practice. But with a little intention, you can do it. Following are some statements your partner might make. Read each separately, listening for feelings beneath the words. Make note of the feelings you "hear" and write out a response that reflects the feelings behind each of the statements (see examples). We're just giving you five of these to try, so it won't take long to do.

EXAMPLES

Statement: *"Just once I'd like to not have to pick your coat off this chair."*

Reflection of feeling: *"That has to be irritating, I know. I'll do my best to break that habit."*

Statement: *"I can't believe you agreed to go to this event tonight without asking me first."*

Reflection of feeling: *"Sounds like you're feeling betrayed."*

1. **"I don't want your advice!"**

_____

_____

_____

2. **"Wendy used to email or phone me, but I haven't heard from her in ages."**

_____

_____

_____

3. **"You need to call me if you're running late so I know what's going on."**

_____

_____

_____

4. **"I'm not sure what to do about my manager at work. He's so unreasonable with his deadlines."**

_____

_____

_____

5. **"There is no way I'm going to let my mother spoil this party by rearranging the seats at the table this year."**

_____

_____

_____

Now compare your reflective statements to those listed below to see how accurately you recognized the possible feelings. Give yourself a 2 on those items where your reflection closely matches, a 1 on items where your reflection only partially matches, and a 0 if you missed the mark altogether.

POSSIBLE RESPONSES

1. "Sounds like you'd just like to be understood."

2. "You must feel kind of hurt by that."

3. "You must get frustrated when you don't know I'm running late—I need to remember to call you."

4. "Sounds like you're really feeling pressured at work."

5. "You sound pretty determined to set boundaries."

How you rate on "hearing" the feelings beneath the words:

SCORE

8–10   Above average recognition of feelings

5–7   Average recognition of feelings

0–4   Below average recognition of feelings

Don't get hung up on how you rated in this exercise. The point is to better reflect the feelings of your partner.

The point of reflective listening is to let your partner know you've heard what they have said and you understand their message. By the way, reflective listening is a wonderful way to defuse a potential conflict. If your partner starts hurling "you" statements, such as "You are always late," don't say, "I am not." Instead, genuinely express your understanding of their feelings by saying, "I know it upsets you when I'm late. It must be exasperating. I'll work on being on time in the future." Listen for the message underlying the actual words. "You are always late" means "I'm upset."

Renowned Swiss counselor Dr. Paul Tournier said, "It is impossible to overemphasize the immense need we have to be really listened to, to be taken seriously, to be understood. . . . No one can develop freely in this world and find a full life without feeling understood by at least one person."[2] When you offer your spouse the gift of listening, you are embodying what marriage was meant to be.

 Do you agree that having your spouse reflect feelings that may not be blatantly stated can be helpful? Why or why not? How do you each feel about your capacity to do so?

COMMUNICATION SKILLS YOU'D LIKE TO IMPROVE

At the bottom of this page of your SYMBIS+ Report, you've each indicated three specific ways you'd like to improve when it comes to communication. Fantastic! You're already ahead of most couples. You've identified a skill or a strategy that will not only improve communication but strengthen your marriage. If you haven't already explored why you chose these items and what you will do in practical terms to make them happen, be sure to do so.

The following exercise will take your efforts in this area to an even deeper level—with more return on your investment.

The Five Realms of Communication

At the beginning of this chapter, we took a look at how you're doing when it comes to the basics of communication and we also explored how you can make time for meaningful conversations. In this final communication exercise, we want you to consider the following five realms of communication and indicate on each of the scales where you see yourself. Be thoughtful and honest as you answer.

Information Sharing: Stating your thoughts and feelings with accuracy and clarity without getting sidetracked or embroiled in emotion.

WEAK									STRONG
1	2	3	4	5	6	7	8	9	10

Listening: Paying respectful attention to the words and feelings of another in a way that they know they have been accurately understood.

WEAK									STRONG
1	2	3	4	5	6	7	8	9	10

Conflict Management: Being aware of conflict and employing methods to defuse it and move beyond it.

WEAK									STRONG
1	2	3	4	5	6	7	8	9	10

Problem Solving: Working out effective steps with another to efficiently reach a desired state.

WEAK									STRONG
1	2	3	4	5	6	7	8	9	10

Skill Selection: Determining which communication skills are most useful at specific times.

WEAK									STRONG
1	2	3	4	5	6	7	8	9	10

Once you have rated yourself on each of these five scales you may want to have your partner rate you on these same items. Why? Because their input will likely heighten your self-awareness as you begin to pinpoint even more accurately your communication goals.

Finally, consider what you have just done in the above exercise and the information from this page of your SYMBIS+ Report and write down the first goal you'd like to accomplish when it comes to being a better communicator with your spouse. Be specific. The more specific, the better.

My top communication goal:

_____

_____

_____

Now that you have put your specific goal in writing, be aware of the huge step you have just taken. Only a very small percentage of people put their goals in writing—but those who do are more than twice as likely to reach them as those who just talk about them. And what's more, those who review their goals from time to time are ten times more likely to achieve them. So consider putting this goal on a card or a sticky note and placing it where you will see it over the next few days.

 How are you feeling about what you've learned about communication in this chapter and within your SYMBIS+ Report?

We have one more tip for you before concluding this chapter: Be aware you can do a lot of things very well when it comes to communication, but your conversations can still derail. Why? Because of simple misunderstandings.

When this happens, try a little exercise we call "Let Me Read Your Mind." Don't worry, it doesn't require you to sit on the floor swami style and wear a funny hat. When either one of you is running the risk of reading something into a message that isn't there, say, "I'd like to read your mind." When your partner agrees, tell them what it is you are hearing. Don't pass judgment at this point; just reveal what you perceive. In other words, you're not giving validity to the message at this point; you're just seeing if it's correct. Next, your partner simply rates how accurate you are on a 1 to 10 scale—10 being right on the money.

Here's an example:

She: "I'd like to read your mind."

He: "Be my guest."

She: "Last night at dinner when you made that joke about the number of minutes I used on my cell phone, you were thinking that I spend too much time talking to my sister. Am I right?"

He: "That's about a three. The thought went through my head, but not for long. I was really wondering if we should get a new phone plan if you use that many minutes every month."

Or consider an example of a couple who is thinking about a major move across the country because of a new job offer:

He: "I'd like to read your mind."

She: "Okay."

He: "I think that even though you say you are willing to move our family to Philadelphia, you really want to stay put. I think you're afraid of disappointing me or holding my career back. Am I right?"

She: "Yes. That's about an eight or nine. You're right. I'm afraid to speak up about the situation because I know you're excited about this opportunity."

You get the idea. This little exercise cuts through all the smoke and mirrors of a relationship shrouded by misinterpreted messages. It allows you to put your fears and frustrations on the table to see if they're valid. Think of the time and energy you can save with this technique! But remember, it will fall flat if you're not operating from a base of genuinely wanting to understand your partner.

Chapter 13

GENDER

Wherever people of different sexes gather, there are
bound to be stress fractures along gender lines.

—Deborah Tannen

An inherent completeness occurs when a man and woman marry. Our partner makes up for what we lack. When we are discouraged, they are hopeful. When we are stingy, they are generous. When we are weak, they are strong. Because we are male and female joined together, there is wholeness. But our differences, if not understood and accepted, can become a source of confusion rather than completeness.

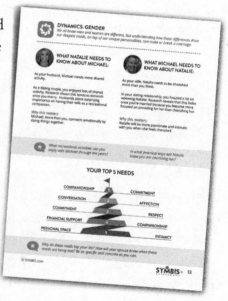

Too often in marriage, the fundamental differences between women and men are overlooked when we mistakenly assume that our partner is just like us—"what is good for me is good for you." We evaluate their behavior according to our feminine or masculine standards, never considering the vast differences between the sexes.

Men and women don't necessarily want to discuss the same subjects. According to a poll of one thousand adults, the leading discussion subject for men was news events (71 percent of respondents), followed by work (68 percent). Women, on the other hand, talked about food (76 percent) and health (72 percent).

What's more, when men and women refer to "conversation," they might not be talking about the same thing at all. Communication theorist Deborah Tannen reports a study where students recorded casual conversations between women friends and men friends. It was easy to get recordings of women friends talking, partly because the request to "record a conversation with your friend" met with easy compliance from the students' female friends and family members. But asking men to record conversations with their friends had mixed results. One woman's mother agreed readily, but her father insisted that he didn't have conversations with his friends.

"Don't you ever call Fred on the phone?" she asked, naming a man she knew to be his good friend.

"Not often," he said. "But if I do, it's because I have something to ask, and when I get the answer, I hang up."

Another woman's husband delivered a tape to her with great satisfaction and pride. "This is a good conversation," he announced, "because it's not just him and me shooting the breeze, like, 'Hi, how are you? I saw a good movie the other day,' and stuff. It's a problem-solving task. Each line is meaningful."

> Your willingness to accept the differences between you will allow you to complement one another in ways that make life better for each of you.
>
> —C. W. Neal

When the woman listened to the tape, she heard her husband and his friend trying to solve a computer problem. Not only did she not consider it "a good conversation," she didn't really regard it as a conversation at all. His idea of a good conversation was one with factual, task-focused content. Hers was one with emotional connection.

And so it goes. For centuries, no doubt, long before "gender studies" were even conceived, men and women have been puzzled by each other. That's why we kick off this chapter with an exercise that simply helps you take inventory of the roles you are each fulfilling as husband and wife in your marriage.

The Roles We Play

Unconsciously or by choice, we all play certain roles in our marriage. This exercise will help you take a bit of a bird's-eye view of the roles you both play, consciously and unconsciously, in your relationship. Complete the following sentences as honestly as you can.

I am important to our marriage because: _____

_____

What I contribute to my partner's success is: _____

_____

I feel central to our relationship when: _____

_____

I feel peripheral to our relationship when: _____

_____

The ways I have fun with you are: _____

_____

The way I get space for myself in our relationship is: _____

_____

The ways I am intimate with you are: _____

_____

The role I play as your husband/wife is: _____

_____

I feel most masculine/feminine in our relationship when: _____

_____

I deal with stress by: _____

_____

The division of labor for household tasks is decided by: _____

_____

Our finances are controlled by: _____

_____

How we spend our spare time is determined by: _____

_____

Our social life is planned by: _____

_____

I need you to: _____

_____

As you review the statements you've written, consider how they have shaped and are shaping the roles you both fulfill in your relationship. Compare your statements and discuss how your gender impacts the way you responded.

What roles have you naturally fallen into in your marriage simply because of your gender and how do you feel about them? Anything the two of you would like to change?

WHAT YOU NEED TO KNOW ABOUT EACH OTHER

Whenever we conduct a marriage retreat, we often have a session where we divide the group for a brief discussion—wives in one circle, husbands in another. We then ask a question that always generates a lively conversation among the groups: What do men need to know about women, and what do women need to know about men? The responses are predictable:

MEN SAY . . .	WOMEN SAY . . .
• Women are too emotional	• Men aren't sensitive enough
• Women don't feel as much pressure to provide the family's income	• Men don't do their fair share of the housework
• Women frequently deny their real power	• Men are afraid to be vulnerable or out of control
• Women talk too much	• Men don't listen

The point of the discussion is not to gripe about the opposite sex but to help *couples* see, first of all, that there are predictable differences between the sexes, and second, to realize that the differences they thought were personal, strictly between them and their spouse, are often shared by most other *couples*. "I thought we were marriage mutants before this exercise," one *couple* told us. "Just realizing how universal our differences are lets us know we are normal and can make it work."

At the top of this page of your SYMBIS+ Report you've discovered some fundamental gender differences. Have you discussed them?

 Do you agree or disagree with the top section of this page of your report? Why?

Whatever your gender differences are and regardless of how wide the gap, the solution is always the same: empathy. We've talked about the value of empathy in previous chapters but when it comes to bridging the gender gap it bears repeating. Putting yourself in each other's shoes is the best and quickest way to overcome any issues that are keeping you from connecting.

Bring On the Empathy

This is a bit of a visualization exercise to help you see the world more clearly from your partner's perspective. Ready? You may want to close your eyes for parts of it. In fact, once you've read through this, try closing your eyes and seeing yourself, in your mind's eye, as your partner. Do your best to imagine what it would be like to live in their skin. Take a good sixty seconds or more to ponder this.

Next, consider a typical day and ask yourself the following questions. We've provided space under each one of them for you to jot a little note so that you can later compare your thoughts with your partner's.

On a typical day as your partner . . .

What time did you get up in the morning, and how did you sleep? What's your morning mood like and why?

_____

_____

_____

How long would it take you to get ready for the day? Would you spend more or less time in front of the mirror? What would you wear?

_____

_____

_____

When would you leave the house, if you left at all? What would your activities throughout the day be?

_____

_____

What would you worry about in a typical day? What would be your likely stress points?

_____

_____

_____

What would bring you the greatest joy or satisfaction during a typical day?

_____

_____

_____

Would you have different financial responsibilities or pressures?

_____

_____

_____

Would you eat differently? Exercise differently? Would you be more or less concerned about your physical appearance?

_____

_____

_____

Would you feel more or less self-assured?

_____

_____

_____

How would you feel toward the end of the day as you're getting ready for dinner? What would be on your mind?

_____

_____

_____

And how would you feel about your partner (that would be you!)? What would you want most from your partner? How would you communicate with your partner?

_____

_____

_____

Now discuss your experience with your partner and review your notes together.

You undoubtedly have a unique and fresh perspective on life in your partner's skin after doing this exercise. Now take a few minutes to review your experience with your partner. Compare notes and invite feedback about your take on life as your partner.

What is the main insight you gained about your partner after doing this visualization exercise? How will it give you more empathy in your relationship?

When you consider all the gender differences relevant to communication between the sexes and try to make sense of them, you will invariably risk oversimplification. We admit that we run this risk. But the risk is worth it. Albert Einstein once said, "Make everything as simple as possible, but not simpler." That's our goal here. So we'll temper our analogies and refrain from comments about men and women being from different planets, or food groups, or species. We choose, instead, to just say it like it is: Men analyze. Women sympathize. It's as simple—and difficult—as that.

Not only are men's and women's brains different, but the way we use them differs dramatically. Neuropsychologist Ruben Gur of the University of Pennsylvania used brain scan tests to show that when a man's brain is in a resting state, less than 30 percent of its electrical activity is active. Scans of women's brains showed 90 percent activity during the same state, confirming that women are constantly receiving and analyzing information from their environment.

For most women, it's obvious when another person is upset or feeling hurt, while a man generally has to physically witness tears or a temper tantrum before he even has a clue that anything is wrong. What is commonly called "women's intuition" is mostly a woman's acute ability to notice small details and changes in the appearance or behavior of others. And this aptitude enhances a woman's sympathetic ability (her personal fear factor of losing approval can heighten this).

But while women have a near sixth sense for small details, their eyesight seems to change drastically when it comes to backing a car into a garage. Estimating the distance between the car fender and the garage wall while moving is, after all, a spatial skill located mainly in the right front hemisphere in men—an aptitude enhancing a man's analytic ability.

> I am a man and you are a woman. I can't think of a better arrangement.
> —Groucho Marx

The differences between the genders can go on and on. And in about 10 percent of couples, the generalized differences between the genders can actually be reversed. That's why we won't belabor the point. And that's also why the second half of your SYMBIS+ Report concludes with a list of your top five needs. Be sure you review these needs—even if you've already done so with your SYMBIS Facilitator. Use them as a means to better empathize with each other. Understand one another's needs by asking each other questions about them.

Which of your partner's top five needs do you understand the most? Which one do you understand the least? Why? How can you understand it better?

Chapter 14

CONFLICT

The course of true love never did run smooth.

—Shakespeare

We were traveling in Beijing, China, one summer a few years ago and were invited to the humble home of some villagers outside the city. Through an interpreter, Les commented on the bright red paper decorations around the small door frame of the otherwise drab two-room home. His remark delighted the husband and wife, in their eighties, who lived there.

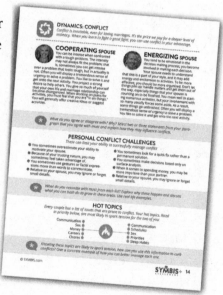

As they invited us in, our hosts bowed repeatedly and directed us to a wooden table that looked about as old as they were. The home was dimly lit by a single, exposed light bulb. It was hot and humid. The air was stagnant and stale. They offered us hand-held fans which we gladly accepted. Without much talking, but speaking a few words in broken English, they proceeded to demonstrate the ancient art of *jianzhi*, Chinese paper cutting. In the process, they gave us each a pair of surprisingly modern scissors and a thin sheet of bright red paper, asking us to follow their direction. We set aside our handheld fans, carefully folded, and then cut with meticulous precision into the red paper to fashion a mysterious Chinese symbol.

After dozens and dozens of tiny cuts, we both unfolded our work. "What is it?" Les asked.

"It is a special symbol," our hosts said through the interpreter. Knowing we had written marriage books, he said, "It is used only at weddings. It symbolizes 'double happiness.'"

We nodded and smiled. Then Les cracked a joke meant just for me about how you'd need some kind of double reward after working so diligently to make such an intricate symbol. That led to some lighthearted teasing between us about which one of us had done a better job of creasing and cutting the paper.

Observing this exchange and knowing only a few English words, our hosts thought we were actually having a little tiff.

Thankfully, our interpreter explained our playful banter, letting them know we were just having fun.

"The husband wants you to know that we have a saying in China," our interpreter told us: "Even the teeth sometimes bite the tongue."

Before we could ask for an explanation, our hosts were giggling in delight. And then this wise husband slowly said, "Even loving couple have war." We all burst into laughter. The spirit of his message was clear. He was stating a marriage truth that transcends oceans and national boundaries: even in the closest and most loving of relationships we sometimes have painful moments when "the teeth bite the tongue."

> Marriage is nature's way of keeping us from fighting with strangers.
> —Alan King

Conflict. It's pervasive, recurring, and universal. That's why this page of your SYMBIS+ Report is vital. All couples fight. Fighting is as intrinsic to marriage as sex. And the goal for both is to do them well.

Hear this: What matters is *how* we fight, not *whether* we fight. Couples who stay happily married disagree just as much as the couples who get divorced. But they've learned how to use those disagreements to deepen their connection. They've built a bridge over issues that would otherwise divide them. Above all, happily married couples see each other as allies, not adversaries.

Allies or Adversaries?

Not all fights are created equal. A "good fight," in contrast to a "bad fight," is helpful, not hurtful. It's positive, not negative. A good fight stays clean while a bad fight gets dirty. And 93 percent of couples who fight dirty will be divorced in ten years, according to researchers at the University of Utah.[1] A study at Ohio State University showed that unhealthy marital arguments contribute significantly to a higher risk of heart attacks, headaches, back pain, and a whole slew of problems—not to mention unhappiness.[2] In the end, bad fights lead to marriages that are barely breathing and eventually die. In fact, researchers can now predict with 94 percent accuracy whether a couple will stay together or not based solely on *how* they fight.[3] Not *whether* they fight, but *how* they fight.

To help you fight a good fight—to help you become allies more than adversaries—consider this chart that distinguishes a good fight from a bad fight. Circle one value in each row below to note which approach you think you lean into most. As always, be as honest with yourself as you can (having in mind a couple of specific conflicts you've had with your spouse is helpful as you do this):

	BAD FIGHT	GOOD FIGHT
Goal	Win the fight	Resolve the fight
Topic	Surface issues	Underlying issues
Emphasis	Personalities and power struggles	Ideas and issues
Attitude	Confrontational and defensive	Cooperative and receptive
Motivation	Shift blame	Take responsibility
Mode	Belittle	Respect
Manner	Egocentric	Empathic
Demeanor	Self-righteous	Understanding
Side effect	Escalation of tension	Easing of tension
Result	Discord	Harmony
Benefit	Stagnation and distance	Growth and intimacy

So which column has more boxes circled—the bad fight or the good fight column? As you review the distinctives between the two kinds of fights, answer the following:

What are some specific examples that support why I answered the way I did—especially for the "good fight" column?

_____

_____

_____

From the "bad fight" column, which item do you want to change the most and why?

_____

_____

_____

What can you do, in specific terms, to ensure that your fights with your spouse are more good than bad?

_____

_____

_____

Compare how you and your spouse answered these items and discuss what you can learn from your responses.

 When it comes to inevitable conflict with your spouse, do you generally feel more like allies or adversaries? Why?

YOUR FIGHT TYPES

A man from Berlin, Germany, took an unusual approach in trying to bring peace to his marriage. *CNN* reported that the man was using an old air raid siren to stun his wife into submission.

"My wife never lets me get a word in edgeways," the man identified as Vladimir R. told the police. "So I crank up the siren and let it rip for a few minutes. It works every time. Afterward, it's real quiet again."

The seventy-three-year-old man's 220-volt rooftop siren was confiscated by police after neighbors filed complaints. As for his wife of thirty-two years, she said "My husband is a stubborn mule, so I have to get loud."[4]

You might say this couple has "issues." Right? Truth be told, we all do. Thankfully, most of us don't resort to blaring sirens to get through to our spouse. We use subtler ways of communicating. In fact, now that you have read through the paragraphs at the top of this page of your SYMBIS+ Report, you should have a far clearer understanding of how each of you is hardwired to manage conflict. With the guidance of your SYMBIS Facilitator you've probably already explored what sentences you resonate with most and least. That's great. But revisit that conversation with your spouse for a moment and talk about how you can take this information even deeper—to a more practical level.

 What does your spouse's paragraph reveal about their "fight type" that you never really considered before, and how can this new insight help you manage conflict better? Be specific and concrete.

PERSONAL CONFLICT CHALLENGES

You've likely already considered your conflict challenges when it comes to fighting a good fight with your partner. Your SYMBIS Facilitator has had you review your personal list of challenges on the SYMBIS+ Report.

Regardless of what is on your list of challenges, we can all benefit from knowing when it's time to fight—or not. In other words, we all need to know when it might be best to take a time-out before the fight begins. Why? Because for a good fight to occur, you both need to be ready.

"Let's get ready to rumble!" You need to read that sentence in a loud, long-drawn-out voice for full effect. Michael Buffer, a professional ring announcer for boxing and professional wrestling, made this his catchphrase starting in the early 1980s. He has a way of rolling certain letters and adding inflection that is so unique he literally acquired a federal trademark for the phrase. He even used a variation of it for a Kraft Cheese commercial in which he says, "Let's get ready to *crumble*!"

It's not a bad distinction for our purposes. Sometimes when faced with a conflictual topic we are more ready to crumble than rumble. A bad fight always leads to crumbling. A good rumble, however, is another story. The question is, how do you know whether a conflict will be a good rumble?

> Coming together is the beginning.
> Keeping together is progress.
> Working together is success.
>
> —Henry Ford

Readiness can be tricky. When a verbal skirmish hijacks our conversation and we're about to get embroiled in conflict, we don't typically stop and ask ourselves if we're ready for it. It just happens—ready or not.

But what would happen if right in that moment you could quickly know whether or not you were ready to rumble? What if you could immediately determine whether the fight would be good or bad?

Truth be told, you can. If you're emotionally amped up or if you're irritable and hungry or if you're PMS-ing, you're bound to have a bad fight. The odds are stacked against you. On top of that, some of us with a more aggressive personality may even trick ourselves into believing we're ready for a fight when we're not.

Here's our simple checklist for deciding if you're ready or not. If you agree with any of the following statements during the conflictual moment, you're not ready to fight.

- ☐ I'm hungry or in pain.
- ☐ I'm tired or exhausted.
- ☐ I'm emotionally charged.
- ☐ I'm pressed for time or need to think.

It only takes one of these statements to spoil a good fight. And when they occur, it's time to take a time out.

Taking a Timeout?

There are times when the best way to move forward with friction is simply to stop talking about whatever is causing the problem. Consider the following four scenarios and determine which of them are situations to talk about and which are issues to clam up on. We've provided three options under each scenario. Be honest about what you would do in each situation.

Your partner is dying to delve into what you are thinking about a potential job change, but you aren't quite ready to talk about it because you know it's going to be intense. What do you do?

> **A.** Talk about it anyway.
>
> **B.** Say, "Honestly, I don't know when I'll ever be ready to get into that conversation with you."
>
> **C.** Say, "I need some more time to think about this, but I'll be ready to talk after dinner tonight."

You and your partner have had the same conversation a million times about whether to drive a used car and be debt-free *or* buy a brand-new vehicle and carry debt. After countless attempts to find common ground, you know you're highly unlikely to see eye to eye on the issue anytime soon. So when your spouse brings it up again, you are most likely to:

> **A.** Rationally try one more time to make your case and convince your spouse to finally agree with you.
>
> **B.** Get emotional and say how blatantly wrong your partner is to believe that way.
>
> **C.** Refuse to talk about it or even mention it for at least a month.

You are trying to decide with your partner whether to attend a party that likely will be boring but may be an opportunity to network with people who can open up some doors for you. You're exhausted and don't want to go. Suddenly, your partner goes into a tirade and gets overly emotional, even

irrational, saying how lazy you are and how unthinkable it would be not to attend. You are most likely to:

> **A.** Come back with equal emotion about how unthinkable it is for them to put this kind of pressure on you.
>
> **B.** Say, "Do you have any idea how ridiculous you sound right now?"
>
> **C.** Say, "I'm going to give you some space for a few minutes, and then we can talk after you pull it together."

Your partner is driving home from work and calls to tell you that they were given a huge project that may eat up some of your weekend. You are likely to:

> **A.** Sulk and whine a bit about missing out on some fun stuff you hoped to do during your weekend together.
>
> **B.** Say, "I guess I don't have any say in that." And clam up.
>
> **C.** Say, "I know you didn't ask for my advice, but can I offer a suggestion about how you can get your project done earlier so we can still salvage our weekend?"

Okay. Let's see how you fared. There's no scoring to be done here, because the point of the exercise is simply to give you ideas for when and how to halt a conversation if needed. In each of these scenarios, we propose that the best answer is C. Why? Because this category of answer helps you put on the brakes in a situation that is otherwise likely to run amuck. The remainder of this chapter will expound on these kinds of examples and several others.

As soon as one person in a couple feels too upset or negative to follow healthy problem-solving steps, it's time to take a break. Experts say agreeing ahead of time to take a time-out if one partner becomes overwhelmed is crucial for avoiding a downward spiral you'll only regret later. As Harry Emerson Fosdick said, "No one can get inner peace by pouncing on it."

So here are the essentials for having a productive time out:

- Include in your agreement the understanding that you'll get back to your discussion within twenty-four hours.
- If you're the one ready to blow, stop the conflict by simply saying, "I need a time-out." Some couples use a sports signal, such as the "T" sign coaches use, to indicate they need a break.
- Affirm your intention to solve the problem together later. In other words, don't just leave. Say something like, "I want to resolve this, but I can't right now. I'll let you know when I'm ready."
- Stop the discussion right away and go somewhere you can calm down. It takes at least twenty minutes for the body to slow itself down after being worked up.
- Take a walk, read a book, cook a meal, or take a bath. Don't spend your time ruminating about the conversation or having bad thoughts about your spouse.
- Tell your spouse (even with a text or email) when you will be ready to reengage. Say something like, "I'll be ready to continue in one hour," or "I'll be ready before dinner tonight." Setting a deadline for the timeout to end is essential.
- If possible, before you talk again, try to first share an everyday activity together to re-establish a close, calm connection.

It is impossible to have a rational discussion in a climate of hostility and disrespect. Taking a timeout is one of the easiest ways to rekindle respect for your spouse and keep a fight from escalating. So don't be afraid to cool off, calm down, and gain some perspective when you're overheating.

 Can you see the value in taking a timeout? What can help the two of you to do just that the next time it's needed?

HOT TOPICS

Couples fight about anything and everything. Sometimes the issue is trivial (putting the cap back on the toothpaste), sometimes important (investing money without discussing it first).

We once had a couple in our counseling office who were fighting about whether the chances of a coin toss were truly 50/50. They'd been arguing their respective sides for a couple of days and neither one recognized how insanely silly the argument was. We know another couple who had a fight about what day of the week a specific date fell on the previous year. But the fight that took the cake was the woman in our office who did not like the way her husband breathed. No kidding! Couples sometimes fight about the silliest of issues.

Of course, other fights are about issues we hold near and dear. They are critically important. We might have conflict over how we balance our budget—or how we don't. It might be about whether to have a child or how we discipline the child we have. We might fight about feeling disrespected, slighted, or even betrayed. These are not lighthearted issues. They deserve serious attention and eventual resolution.

As you've reviewed your "Hot Topics" list on the bottom of the Conflict page of your SYMBIS+ Report, you've probably thought of a number of conflicts that may have occurred around each topic. As you think back on them, how would you rate their importance? Wait, don't answer that question just yet. Save it for this exercise.

How Important Is It?

In the heat of marital battle, it can seem like every topic is vitally important. To determine a topic's level of importance, you can consider where on these four scales you might fall for any particular topic of contention.

Think of an issue that has caused or is causing conflict for the two of you (see "Hot Topics" on your SYMBIS+ Report). Have a specific issue in mind? Now place an X on each of the four scales to see how important the matter really is:

Gravity of Outcome: Will the result of this fight really matter?

TRIVIAL   CRITICAL

| 1 | 2 | 3 | 4 | 5 | 6 | 7 | 8 | 9 | 10 |

Level of Hurt/Sadness: Do I feel wounded or down because of it?

NOT HURT/SAD   VERY HURT/SAD

| 1 | 2 | 3 | 4 | 5 | 6 | 7 | 8 | 9 | 10 |

Impact on Values: Is this issue a threat to my convictions or principles?

NONTHREATENING   VERY THREATENING

| 1 | 2 | 3 | 4 | 5 | 6 | 7 | 8 | 9 | 10 |

Preoccupation: How much am I thinking or worrying about it?

NOT THINKING ABOUT IT   OBSESSING ABOUT IT

| 1 | 2 | 3 | 4 | 5 | 6 | 7 | 8 | 9 | 10 |

The more weight you put on the right end of any of these areas, the more important this issue is to you. Next, compare how your spouse rates the importance of this issue.

Can you see the value in gauging how important a particular topic is when you're fighting about it? Can this simple recognition help you determine whether it's worth fighting for or not?

Before concluding this chapter on conflict, we want to share one more strategy that will help the two of you fight more good fights than bad. It's an exercise we've been using in our own marriage for decades. And we've taught it to hundreds of thousands of couples. We call it Sharing Withholds. What will it do for you? It will minimize conflict and increase intimacy. Almost guaranteed.

Sharing Withholds

This exercise will help you and your partner keep a clean emotional slate and avoid needless conflicts. We call it "Sharing Withholds" because it gives you the chance to share thoughts and feelings that you may have withheld from each other. It takes just ten minutes or so and we recommend you do it on a weekly basis.

Begin by writing two things your spouse has done in the last forty-eight hours that you sincerely appreciated but have not told them. For example, "I appreciate the compliment you gave me as I got out of the car yesterday and I never did tell you." Or "I appreciate the help you gave me in writing my proposal last night and I don't think you know how much that meant to me."

Go ahead, write two positive withholds that have happened in the past couple of days:

I appreciate: _____

I appreciate: _____

Next, write one thing your spouse has done in the last forty-eight hours that irritated you but that you didn't say anything about at the time. For example, "I didn't like it when you borrowed my umbrella without telling me" or "I didn't like it when you said nothing about the meal I prepared for us last night."

Write your one negative withhold:

I didn't like it when: _____

Once both of you have written your statements, take turns sharing them. One person shares all three statements one after the other—we recommend sandwiching the negative withhold between the two positives when you share them. Then the other person shares his or her three statements.

And here is an important part of the exercise. The person on the receiving end can say only "Thank you" after each statement. That's all—just "Thank you." This rule allows couples to share something that bugs them without fearing a blow-up or a defensive reaction. It also allows couples to receive critiques in the context of affirmation.

After thirty minutes, if you wish, you can ask your partner questions about the negative withhold and you're sure to experience a far less intense emotional reaction. At that point, too, you may simply be inclined to offer an apology if you like.

The point is not to stir up a fight where there is none. The point is to clear the emotional landmines from your marriage by keeping you current and not allowing painful wounds, even minor ones, to fester.

This exercise can be done every week, as we mentioned. Once you get the hang of it, you don't necessarily need to write down your statements, though doing so may be helpful. You also may want to agree on a routine time when you can do this exercise each week (e.g., Wednesdays after dinner) so one of you doesn't always have to initiate it. If you make this practice a weekly habit, you're sure to see significant payoffs. Sharing withholds can save you hundreds of hours of needless bickering—and deepen your intimacy because you're hearing compliments you've been missing.

 Are the two of you willing to try Sharing Withholds once a week for the next four weeks? Can you agree on a time you will do it so one of you doesn't have to initiate it? When?

An African proverb says, "Smooth seas do not make skillful sailors." It takes a little turmoil for any of us to get really good at something—including our relationship. As we weather tough times together and come out stronger on the other side, we build trust and confidence in our relationship. We find security.

This sounds counterintuitive, but a good fight, as opposed to a bad one, makes a couple's relationship more solid. It empowers us. We begin to realize we don't have to be afraid of troubles and tension. We can work it out. We're strong. *Our love can stand up when it gets knocked around*, we say to ourselves.

> A marriage without conflicts is almost as inconceivable as a nation without crises.
> —Andre Maurois

Chapter 15

SPIRITUALITY

Anyone without a soul friend
is like a body without a head.

—Celtic saying

Robert Sternberg of Yale University studied romantic love long before it was fashionable among scholars. In his groundbreaking project he discovered love's essential ingredients: passion, commitment, and intimacy.[1] Passion is physical. Commitment is willful. And intimacy is emotional. Intimacy is a feeling that says something along the lines of: "You get me and I get you like nobody on the planet." It's the feeling of being deeply in sync with the person you love. It's a feeling of being best friends.[2]

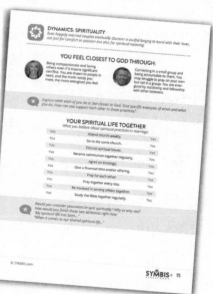

Look up *intimacy* in a dictionary and you'll see words like *close, warm, familiar, affectionate, caring,* and *understanding.* Some researchers say that intimacy emerges when you see less "me" and "you" in the relationship and more "we" and "us."[3] It engenders interdependence, a detailed knowledge of each other, and a deep sense of belonging.[4]

Intimacy involves two criteria, according to a landmark study.[5] First, intimate partners *share information.* They have secrets. They disclose plans and provide personal details that they don't share with others. Second, intimate partners not only share information but *have*

a deep understanding of each other. They know each other's thoughts, habits, and preferences. Mrs. Albert Einstein was once asked if she understood her husband's theory of relativity. "No," she said, "but I know how he likes his tea." That's part of emotional intimacy.

At a meeting for marriage and family therapists some time ago, we heard a speaker define *intimacy* this way: "In-to-me-see." And perhaps that defines the friendship factor of marriage best. Intimacy is seeing into each other's lives. It's being aware of each other's deepest self. It's having a soul-to-soul connection. It's attuning our spirits. Dr. Don Harvey, in *The Spiritually Intimate Marriage*, said it's being able to share your spiritual self, to find this sharing reciprocated, and to enjoy a sense of union. Spiritual intimacy causes a couple's spirits to sprout new wings. Deep and abiding spiritual intimacy empowers a couple's relationship to soar.

What's Your Intimacy Quotient?

Before we get into the spiritual aspects of intimacy and your relationship, let's back up for a moment and help you get a general sense of how well you know each other. Each of you can take the following questionnaire separately. The more honest you are with your answers, the more insightful your results will be.

Yes No I know what stresses my partner currently faces.

Yes No I know the names of people who have been irritating my spouse lately.

Yes No I am very familiar with my partner's religious faith and spiritual quest.

Yes No I can outline my partner's basic philosophy of life.

Yes No I know the most stressful thing that happened to my partner in childhood.

Yes No I can list my partner's major aspirations.

Yes No I have a good sense of my partner's spiritual journey.

Yes No I know what my spouse thinks and feels about God.

Yes No I feel my partner knows me well.

Yes No I feel emotionally connected with my spouse on most days.

No scoring for this one. You can plainly see that the more you answered yes to these statements, the deeper your emotional intimacy with your spouse is likely to be.

 Generally, are you happy and content with the level of intimacy you and your spouse share? What would make it deeper for you?

"Woe to him who is alone when he falls and has not another to lift him up," warns the sage of Ecclesiastes. So true. We need the care that comes from intimacy. Without it, we are sure to be unhappy.

The National Opinion Research Center asked people a simple question: "Looking over the last six months, who are the people with whom you discussed matters important to you?" Compared to those who could name no such intimate, those who could immediately name someone were 60 percent more likely to feel "very happy."[6]

Six massive investigations, each interviewing thousands of people across several years, have all reached a common conclusion: intimacy not only increases happiness but is essential to sustaining it.[7] Those who feel known and understood by family friends, or a close-knit religious community are not only less vulnerable to stress and disease; their wellbeing skyrockets. "Intimate attachments to other human beings," wrote psychiatrist John Bowlby, "are the hub around which a person's life revolves."[8] Feeling close to others with whom we can share intimate thoughts and feelings has two effects, observed the seventeenth-century philosopher Francis Bacon: "It redoubleth joys, and cutteth griefs in half." No doubt about it—intimacy and wellbeing are inextricably linked.

Innumerable medical studies have shown the value of emotional intimacy on recovery, healing, and immunity—not to mention a longer life span. Intimacy, however, is not only good for the body but great for the soul.[9] A growing body of research reveals that people with a personal faith cope more effectively and suffer less depression than those without such a faith.[10] Moreover, believers who incorporate religion into daily living (attending services, reading Scripture, praying), rate higher on two measures of happiness: frequency of positive emotions and overall sense of satisfaction with life.[11]

Why study spirituality in connection to intimacy? Because intimacy wades into the shallow waters of life until spirituality brings it to the deep end. When we reveal our soul to another person—or to God—we are getting to the deep core of intimacy. And stacks upon stacks of research reveal that the more spiritually intimate we feel in our marriage, the happier we are as well.[12]

Your Spiritual Journey

The more you understand each other's personal pilgrimages, the deeper your connection. Part of cultivating spiritual intimacy involves merging two individual journeys. We are all beginners when it comes to spiritual development, but each of us has come from different places and traveled different roads to meet where we are today. You may have grown up in a religious home learning Bible verses, going to Sunday school, and studying at a Christian college. Or maybe you never went to church while growing up and are just becoming grounded in your faith. Whatever your story, take a moment to gather your thoughts about your own spiritual quest. Then make a few notes of some of the significant mile markers.

_____

_____

_____

_____

_____

_____

Now share your journey with your spouse. Reflect on what has brought you to where you are today. Use your time of sharing as a springboard to a deeper discussion of how each of you views spiritual matters.

How would you compare your spiritual journey with your spouse's journey? How are they the same, and how do they differ?

HOW YOU FEEL CLOSEST TO GOD

At the top of this page of your SYMBIS+ Report, you've already explored how each of you feels closest to God. With guidance from your SYMBIS Facilitator, you may have already talked about how your personalities shape your respective relationships with God. Understanding how each partner feels closest to God can be revolutionary for some couples.

Your Sacred Pathways

Gary Thomas, in his helpful book *Sacred Pathways*, describes nine ways we tend to relate to God. Rank the top two or three styles that fit you best. Then try to predict your partner's top pathways before comparing notes.

ME	SPOUSE	
		The Traditionalist loves God through rituals, sacraments, and symbols throughout the year.
		The Visionary loves God by dreaming a great dream to accomplish great things.
		The Socialite loves God best around other people, confiding in them and being accountable to them.
		The Intellectual seeks God with their mind by considering a new theological concept.
		The Caregiver loves God by being compassionate and loving others even if it means significant sacrifice.
		The Contemplative seeks to love God in a quiet pursuit of journaling and reflection.

		The Activist is at war with injustice and loves God by fighting it.
		The Naturalist feels closest to God outdoors in the midst of creation.
		The Worshiper is inspired by joyful celebration and music.

Now jot down some specific ways these styles are manifested in your life. If you are a Contemplative, for example, what do you like to do, where do you like to go, and how much time do you like to spend to be close to God?

_____

_____

_____

Once you and your partner have both noted the top two or three styles that fit you best, spend a few minutes comparing them and discuss what you might learn from each other's pathways.

 How can you celebrate each other's unique sacred pathways and how might you find a new pathway to enjoy together? Be specific.

YOUR SPIRITUAL LIFE TOGETHER

The bulk of this page of your SYMBIS+ Report is devoted to spiritual practices such as prayer. Did you know that couples who pray together . . . well, you know the rest. But it's more than a catchy saying. A University of Chicago survey of married couples found that 75 percent of Americans who pray with their spouses reported their marriages are "very happy" (compared to 57 percent of those who don't). Those who pray together are also more likely to say they respect each other, discuss their marriage together, and—stop the presses—rate their spouses as skilled lovers.[13]

Whether it's a simple grace at dinnertime or some soul-searching meditation, couples routinely say that a shared spiritual life helps keep them close and stokes the fires of emotional intimacy.

But here's a prayer secret most couples don't know: couples who practice meditative prayer are happier overall and feel closer to God than those who practice other kinds of payer, such as petitioning for relief or asking for blessings.[14] Meditative prayer occurs when we simply practice being "in the presence" of God. Brother Lawrence, the Parisian lay brother who worked most of his life in the kitchen of a monastery, literally wrote the book on it. "How happy we would be if we could find the treasure of which the Gospel speaks," he said. "Let us search unceasingly and let us not stop until we have found it." That treasure? To be in relationship with God, of course. So if you don't do so already, consider praying it forward in your relationship. Pray for each other. Pray for your family. Give thanks for your blessings. But don't neglect prayer that simply seeks to have a relationship with God. When you walk together with God, intimacy will find you.

> Unless we think of others and do something for them, we miss one of the greatest sources of happiness.
> —Ray L. Wilbur

How do the two of you feel about prayer in your marriage? What changes would you like to make, if any, regarding prayer in your relationship?

British theologian and acclaimed author C. S. Lewis described happiness fifty years ago in terms that make even more sense today in our fast-paced society:

A car is made to run on [gasoline], and it would not run properly on anything else. Now God designed the human machine to run on himself. He himself is the fuel our spirits were designed to burn, or the food our spirits were designed to feed on. There is no other. That is why it is just no good asking God to make us happy in our own way without bothering about religion. God cannot give us a happiness and peace apart from himself, because it is not there. There is no such thing.[15]

Researchers seem to agree. Survey after survey shows that people with strong religious faith—those who are relating to God—are happier than those who are irreligious.[16] David Myers, a social psychologist at Michigan's Hope College, said that faith provides social support, a sense of purpose, and a reason to focus beyond the self, all of which help root people and lead to greater connection and happiness. And often the most concrete expression of our faith is attending church.

According to sociologist W. Bradford Wilcox of the University of Virginia, married couples who attend church together tend to be happier than couples who rarely or never attend services.[17] Wilcox found that married church-going Americans across denominational and racial classifications were more likely to describe themselves as "very happy" than their nonreligious counterparts. "Attending church only seems to help couples when they attend together," said Wilcox. And he was quick to add that it's not simply attending church that works some kind of magic. "You've got to combine faith and works to enjoy a happy and stable marriage. You need the consistent message, the accountability, and the support a church community can provide to really benefit from religious faith."[18]

 How do the two of you feel about church? What changes would you like to make, if any, regarding the role church plays in your relationship?

"I never knew how selfish I was until I got married," said Gary. After six months of marriage, he was telling us how Paula, his wife, was volunteering at a retirement center one night a week. "At first I resented her being away from me. But a *couple* of months ago she needed a lift, so I went with her." He came back with Paula again and again, until he discovered that helping the older *people* at the center had become the highlight of his week. "It feels good to help others, and it brings Paula and me closer together; it's like we are a team that is making a difference," he told us.

We have heard dozens of similar reports from *couples*. There is something uplifting about reaching out as a team. Almost mystically it becomes bonding. Reaching out to others promotes humility, sharing, compassion, and intimacy in a marriage. Doing good for others helps *couples* transcend themselves and become part of something larger.[19]

Improving Your Service

Here are a few of the ways couples have practiced the fine art of serving others:

- volunteering in a youth group

- supporting someone's education

- taking care of a shut-in's lawn

- welcoming new people to the neighborhood

- doing short-term relief trips overseas

- sending helpful books to people

Take a moment to list a few ways that you and your spouse might reach out together as a team. Work on your own and be as creative as you can before sharing your thoughts with your partner:

_____

_____

_____

Now compare your list with your partner's. Combine your lists and begin to rank the items in order of what both of you might like to do as a team. Once you have a couple of things that seem like they might fit your joint style, discuss in more detail what they might actually look like.

 What do you think might be the best path for the two of you to take in experiencing shared service together? Is there something you might do for someone anonymously that only the two of you would know about?

Chapter 16

TIME STYLES

*Time isn't a commodity, something you pass around
like cake. Time is the substance of life.*

—ANTOINETTE BOSCO

In 1973 a soft song by singer-songwriter Jim Croce plinked out on nearly every radio station in the country. "Time in a Bottle" was the number one hit that autumn. Its sentimental lyrics revealed a heartfelt desire to save every day until eternity passes "just to spend them with you." It spoke of wanting to make the days he had with his wife last forever. And the haunting chorus reminds us that there "never seems to be enough time" with the one you love.

The personal poignancy of Croce's song never could have been predicted upon its release. Just days later, on September 20, 1973, Jim Croce's light aircraft was taking off from a small airstrip in Natchitoches, Louisiana, when the plane snagged a treetop at the end of the dim runway, sending Jim and five others to their deaths.

Ingrid Croce, his wife, was left with only their infant son, who was half-blind, and the heartbreaking legacy of a song she must have heard nearly everywhere she turned that year and every year since. Today, Ingrid owns a restaurant in San Diego, called Croce's, where a giant mural portrait of Jim takes up the back wall. "It serves as an inspiration to me," Ingrid once told a reporter, "to remember how fragile life is and to never ever take for granted the time we have with the one we love."

The significance of time and its tenuous relationship to marriage is felt by nearly every couple. And chances are you feel it, too. We all know that time passes too quickly. If we could save time in a bottle, there's little doubt what we would do with it. And yet the time we do have—the precious time that is given to us each day—is too often frittered away. Squandered. Do you identify?

The Time of Your Life

Rate your current satisfaction level with time in your marriage . . .

UNSATISFIED   SATISFIED

1	2	3	4	5	6	7	8	9	10

Explain: _____

_____

_____

Mario and Melissa, living in the fast lane and dangerously close to a collision, came to see us for counseling. "We feel like strangers," they told us. "We share the same address and sleep in the same bed, but our relationship has become nothing more than a pit stop with a dried-up fuel pump."

Mario and Melissa were running on empty and they knew it. The consequence? Melissa felt isolated and alone and would often say, "I feel like I'm on my own. Mario gets impatient and short with me these days and it makes me withdraw."

Mario, on the other hand, felt burdened and sometimes nagged, saying, "Melissa doesn't understand the pressure I'm under at work and so I've quit talking about it."

They squabbled for a while in our office about balancing childcare while working and so on. They whined and complained about not having enough time. But before the conversation escalated, we intervened by asking, "How will you know when you are maximizing your moments together?" The room fell silent. We handed each of them a pencil and paper and asked them to write their answer.

"I don't need to write it," Mario said as he set the paper aside. "I already have the answer: we'll be maximizing our moments together when we both feel understood and we feel like we're on each other's team."

Melissa agreed. "That's right . . . like we used to be before life got so busy."

We spent the next few minutes making their answer more concrete. We challenged them to identify specific times in the past when they felt like they were on each other's team. We talked about how and when these times happened. They both agreed the experience had to do with feeling fully present with and invested in each other. They didn't want to feel judged or lay blame. They wanted to play tennis together again, laugh more, and so on.

The very process of discussing the positive outcome of maximizing their time seemed to make it more within reach. So why don't you take a moment right now to do the same. Get concrete about what your life together would be like if you were maximizing your moments.

 How will you know when you are maximizing your moments together? What activities will you be doing (or not doing)? How will you feel?

Getting to Know You

One of the telltale signs that our time with each other is slipping into the future is that we unknowingly lose touch. We simply don't know each other the way we once did. Have you ever heard a couple say something like, "We just need some down time to get reacquainted"? Well, this exercise can help you do just that.

Do your best to answer the following questions about your spouse:

What is your spouse's favorite recent movie?

_____

_____

What has your spouse learned about himself or herself in the past year?

_____

_____

What worries your spouse the most right now?

_____

_____

What has your spouse recently been thinking about when it comes to extended family?

_____

_____

What is your spouse most proud of doing in the past month?

_____

_____

What does your spouse like most about you right now?

_____

_____

What is your spouse's favorite childhood memory?

_____

_____

What has touched your spouse most deeply in recent days?

_____

_____

What is the best part of your spouse's day?

_____

_____

Well, can you answer these questions? This is just a start, but these are the kinds of questions that will help you get to know your partner and bring you closer together. Take some time to explore these and other issues together.

When we were both in graduate school and newly married, we lived in a tiny apartment in Southern California. Tucked into the corner of our main room, actually the _only_ room, was a desk with a computer where we spent an inordinate amount of time. Day or night, it seemed, one of us was on that computer working away at a term paper or dissertation. And taped to the top edge of the computer screen was a small piece of paper containing a quote from Abraham Maslow. We placed it in this prominent position where we would see it every day. It read:

> Some people spend their entire lives indefinitely preparing to live.

Why this quote? Because we were beginning six long years of demanding graduate work and we knew we were vulnerable to a deadly trap: putting life on hold until the grueling task was finished. "Once we graduate . . ." was the tempting refrain. "Once we graduate, we'll take a vacation . . . we'll have time to take walks . . . we'll eat better . . . we'll focus on our relationship . . . we'll enjoy life." Of course, you don't have to be earning a PhD to be swindled by this empty attraction.

It can strike and re-strike at any point. After our graduation, the temptation simply evolved: "Once we get a job," or "Once we pay off our student loans," or "Once we buy a house." You get the idea. Like every other couple, we were susceptible to spending our married lives indefinitely preparing to live. We've all been there. If you're honest, you've been tempted to put life on hold, to put off enjoying time together because an important milestone was standing in your way. Or maybe it still is. Any of these sentence stems sound familiar?

Once the kids are older . . .
Once I get my raise . . .
Once we get a new house . . .
Once I quit my job . . .

Or if you haven't put life on hold as you're preparing to live it, maybe you've found yourself on the proverbial "Someday Isle"—a euphemism for the tropical vacation that never materializes. "Someday, I'll have more free time." "Someday, I'll take you on a great trip." "Someday, I'll build that porch we've always wanted." "Someday . . ."

 What are the two of you putting off for "someday"? Or what's currently keeping you from living more fully in the present?

It has been said that the saddest word in our language is "someday." Why? Because "someday" eventually turns into "if only." And "if onlys" are the result of time you can't recoup. "If only we would have made more free time." "If only we would have taken that trip." "If only we would have built that porch." "If only . . ."

It's at that moment—when "someday" becomes "if only"—that your marriage slips quietly into the future and you wonder how you could have let that happen. How could you have taken time, not to mention your relationship, for granted?

YOUR TIME STYLES

Nothing else, perhaps, distinguishes the happiest and most fulfilled couples as much as their tender loving care of time. They spend it wisely. Like uncut diamonds, their times together are precious and they are determined to guard against wasting them. They know that each moment, no matter how fleeting, holds value for them as a couple and they prize the opportunity to make the most of it. They understand what so many couples don't: that only time affords the luxury of creating memories to be cherished. And they are bent on racking up as many memories as possible.

That's why this page of your SYMBIS+ Report is dedicated entirely to helping you understand how each of you is designed for time. Understanding your personal time style, as well as your spouse's, can do more to help you get on the same page with time and reclaim the moments you've been missing together than nearly anything else.

As you can see, your time style is basically determined by how you answer two questions:

1. *How do I relate to time . . . scheduled or unscheduled?*
2. *Which moments in time get most of my attention . . . the present or the future?*

You can see exactly how you answer these two questions by looking at the percentile score you have in each quadrant on this page of your report.

Getting Personal with Your Time Styles

As you review your own time styles chart on your SYMBIS+ Report, consider some real-life examples that demonstrate the various percentiles you have in each quadrant. Simply jot a note or two in each (enough to remind you of the example when you discuss it with your spouse).

Accommodator	Processor
Dreamer	Planner

One of the most common fallacies of time is that you can "find" it. Turn to nearly any business journal or women's magazine and you'll read about ways to "find more time." We talk about time as if it is hidden under the cushion of a chair in our living room or stuck behind a piece of furniture in the basement. The truth is, we'll never find more time. But we can "make" more time. Prioritizing what we want is the key.

Time is made whenever we decide what matters most. A top priority gets more time. If you decide that collecting stamps is the most important thing in your life, you will begin to schedule your day around it. You will spend your money on it. You will talk about it. Because you prioritize it, you'll make decisions that create more time for it. That's why we leave you in this chapter with an exercise that will help you, not find time, but make it.

How to Make More Quality Time

Consider a scenario. You have twenty-four $1 bills in your pocket. Each of them represents an hour in your day. As each hour elapses, you turn in one of your bills. Which hour is the best deal? In other words, which hour was best spent? Which hour was well worth it? Did it involve your spouse? Your kids? If not, that's fine. Maybe it was something exciting at work. Or maybe it was a precious hour of sleep you especially needed. If you use this scenario to reflect on how you spent your time yesterday, which hour would you say was best spent?

_____

_____

_____

Now consider some time that you didn't experience in the past day. Is there something you would have enjoyed doing with your spouse? Something you didn't get to do because there wasn't enough time? It may have been as simple as checking in with each other for a few minutes to discuss the day. Or it may have been lingering over coffee. Or working in the garden together. Or taking a long walk. Note it here:

_____

_____

_____

Next, consider how many of your twenty-four dollars you'd be willing to sacrifice tomorrow for that time you missed out on with your spouse today. In other words, how much time are you willing to sacrifice from other activities in order to have more of that kind of time you just noted above? Would it take making another ten minutes in your day? Twenty minutes? Another hour or two? Determine the amount of time you need to make for the activity you noted above. Write that amount of time here:

_____

_____

_____

Okay. Now that you've determined the amount of quality time you'd like to make, the only thing left is to decide where in your day you are going to take that time from. What are your options? Is it the time it takes to prepare dinner? The time you spend on errands? The time you spend watching TV or reading the paper? Cleaning house? Volunteering? Resting on the couch? Or is it some of your sleep time? Identify the time you'd be willing to sacrifice tomorrow in order to have the quality time you crave with your spouse and write it here:

_____

_____

_____

Now, to help you better empathize with your spouse on this exercise, consider what you think might be the most difficult sacrifice they would have to make (from their perspective) to have more quality time with you and write it here:

_____

_____

_____

Check in with your spouse to see how accurate you are. If you're way off, that's okay. The point is to empathize by seeing time from your partner's perspective.

There you have it. To make more quality time, you have to give up time you are now giving to secondary causes. It's that simple. And that difficult. It's a sacrifice. But that's what priorities are all about—sacrificing something else you might enjoy for the greater good. Robert McKain said, "The reason most goals are not achieved is that we spend our time doing second things first." It ultimately comes down to your choices. And one of the best choices you can make is to do first things first tomorrow—and every day—in your marriage.

 What is the most valuable takeaway you've received from this section on time? How will you have more quality time together because of it?

Chapter 17

HARMONY

There is no remedy for love but to love more.

—Henry David Thoreau

In 1937 a researcher at Harvard University began a study on what factors contribute to human wellbeing and happiness. The research team selected 268 Harvard students who seemed healthy and well-adjusted to be part of what is called a longitudinal study, which means that the researchers would study the lives of these people not just at one point in time but over a period of time. In this case, the period of time has been extraordinary—more than seventy years. It's one of the most in-depth and important studies of our time. With decades of perspective, the study gives a comprehensive view of what affects the level of health and happiness over a lifetime.

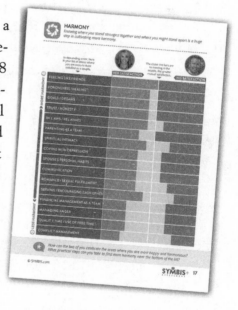

The study has tracked an array of factors, including physical exercise, cholesterol levels, marital status, the use of alcohol, smoking, education level, and weight, but also more subjective psychological factors such as how a person employs defense mechanisms to deal with the challenges of life.

Over the last forty-two years, the director of this study has been psychiatrist George Vaillant. In 2008 someone asked Dr. Vaillant what he had learned about human health

169

and happiness from his years of poring over the data on these people. You would expect a complex answer from a Harvard social scientist, but his secret to happiness was breathtakingly simple: "The only thing that really matters in life are your relationships."[1]

That's it: relationships. The most in-depth study ever conducted on the wellbeing of human beings sums up what matters most for our health and happiness with that single word. It's not surprising, really. As researchers have pursued the age-old mystery of what makes people happy, what appears consistently at the top of the charts is not success, wealth, achievement, good looks, or any of those enviable assets. It's always *relationships*. Close ones. In fact, marriage is the centerpiece of close relationships. For it's in the context of marriage that our deepest needs can be met, as long as the relationship is harmonious.

> There is little difference in people, but that little difference makes a big difference.
>
> —W. Clement Stone

So we conclude this guidebook as well as the SYMBIS+ Report with Harmony. This page of your report, as you know, gives you a customized ranking of some of the most salient issues in any marriage relationship: from the most harmonious issues at the top of your list to the least harmonious at the bottom.

 In reviewing your customized list, what surprised you the most and why?

No doubt you've already gone over your list with your SYMBIS Facilitator. You have already high-fived on the issues where you're doing well. And hopefully you're beginning to chart a course for what you can do to improve the areas that need the most improving. We dedicated this chapter to giving you exercises and tools that will help you do just that.

Taking Inventory

Consider where you land on five dimensions for improving your relationship. These dimensions are what most professionals will tell you are needed for maximizing your marital success. You'll rate them first for yourself.

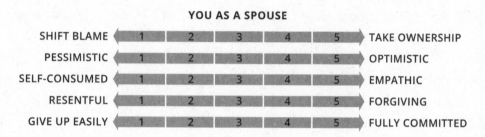

YOU AS A SPOUSE

	1	2	3	4	5	
SHIFT BLAME						TAKE OWNERSHIP
PESSIMISTIC						OPTIMISTIC
SELF-CONSUMED						EMPATHIC
RESENTFUL						FORGIVING
GIVE UP EASILY						FULLY COMMITTED

Now do the same thing for your partner. Indicate your perception of where your spouse stands on the same qualities. Be as objective as you can and consider your reasoning behind each ranking.

YOUR SPOUSE

	1	2	3	4	5	
SHIFT BLAME						TAKE OWNERSHIP
PESSIMISTIC						OPTIMISTIC
SELF-CONSUMED						EMPATHIC
RESENTFUL						FORGIVING
GIVE UP EASILY						FULLY COMMITTED

After both you and your partner have rated these qualities on your own, take a few minutes to discuss your results. Be sure to stay objective and receptive in this discussion. Begin by simply sharing where each of you rank yourselves, then turn to your perception of each other. Be sensitive to your partner's feelings and be open to what your partner has to say. The goal is to learn what both of you bring to your joint efforts in learning to improve your relationship and grow together as a couple.

What one or two actionable items can you take away from this exercise? In other words, what will you do, personally, to help improve the state of your marriage?

A few steps from our offices you can cross a canal that joins Puget Sound to Lake Washington and walk down a trail that will take you to the University of Washington. It's on this campus that some of the most groundbreaking research on marriage has ever been conducted. In 1986, Dr. John Gottman founded a research laboratory with funding from the National Institute of Mental Health where he used video, heart rate monitors and measures of pulse amplitude to code the behavior and physiology of hundreds of couples at different points in their relationship. He has done more yeoman work on conflict in marriage than anyone we know. And over lunch one day at a picturesque restaurant between our two campuses, we asked John what single quality was most detrimental to a couple's growth and wellbeing.

Dr. Gottman didn't have to think twice. "It's contempt," he said. "Contempt is so lethal to love that it ought to be outlawed." He went on to tell us how predictive contempt is of turmoil and even eventual divorce for a couple. Contempt is any belittling remark that makes your spouse feel about an inch tall. It's often sarcastic: "Way to go, Einstein, you're a regular genius." In fact, it doesn't even have to be spoken. Dr. Gottman told us that even when a spouse rolls their eyes at their partner it's toxic. Contempt conveys disdain, disapproval, and dishonor. In short, contempt conveys disrespect.

Everyone wants respect. Scratch that. We *need* respect. We can't have a relationship without it. An attitude of respect builds a bridge of trust between a husband and wife even when they are feeling at odds. Respect does more than curb contempt, however. It helps us listen before speaking. It drives us to understand before passing judgment.

Showing R-E-S-P-E-C-T

Take a moment to rate the following statements on each of the scales below. They will give you a quick idea where you stand on respecting yourself and your partner. Take your time and be honest.

I honor my partner's decisions.

RARELY				MUCH OF THE TIME					ALWAYS
1	2	3	4	5	6	7	8	9	10

I feel proud to be with my partner.

RARELY				MUCH OF THE TIME					ALWAYS
1	2	3	4	5	6	7	8	9	10

I believe our relationship is great because of my partner.

RARELY				MUCH OF THE TIME					ALWAYS
1	2	3	4	5	6	7	8	9	10

I sincerely appreciate what my partner brings to our relationship.

RARELY				MUCH OF THE TIME					ALWAYS
1	2	3	4	5	6	7	8	9	10

I feel very secure in my partner's commitment to me.

RARELY				MUCH OF THE TIME					ALWAYS
1	2	3	4	5	6	7	8	9	10

I really prize how special my partner is.

RARELY				MUCH OF THE TIME					ALWAYS
1	2	3	4	5	6	7	8	9	10

I believe I am doing the very best I can as a partner.

RARELY				MUCH OF THE TIME					ALWAYS
1	2	3	4	5	6	7	8	9	10

I know I'm deeply loved by my partner.

RARELY				MUCH OF THE TIME					ALWAYS
1	2	3	4	5	6	7	8	9	10

I make sure my own needs (as well as my partner's) get met.

RARELY				MUCH OF THE TIME					ALWAYS
1	2	3	4	5	6	7	8	9	10

I have confidence in my ability to make good decisions.

RARELY				MUCH OF THE TIME					ALWAYS
1	2	3	4	5	6	7	8	9	10

I know I'm still worthwhile even when I disappoint my partner.

RARELY				MUCH OF THE TIME					ALWAYS
1	2	3	4	5	6	7	8	9	10

I'm not afraid to speak my mind, and I don't sweep my feelings under the rug.

RARELY				MUCH OF THE TIME					ALWAYS
1	2	3	4	5	6	7	8	9	10

SCORING

Add up your score for items 1 through 6. This is your partner-respect score.

Next, tally your answers for items 7 through 12. This is your self-respect score.

Partner-respect score: ____   Self-respect score: ____

Now compare your scores with each other. Unpack any of the items you'd like to explore further.

Do you agree that respect is essential to your marriage? What did you learn about respect in your relationship from this exercise? How might that insight help you create more harmony together?

One of the subtle saboteurs of harmony in marriage is unfinished business. All of us, at least unconsciously, marry in the hope of healing our wounds. Even if we don't have a traumatic background, we still have hurts and unfulfilled needs that we carry inside. We all suffer from feelings of self-doubt, unworthiness, and inadequacy. No matter how nurturing our parents were, we never received enough attention and love. So in marriage we look to our spouse to convince us that we are worthwhile and to heal our infirmities.[2]

In *Getting the Love You Want*, pastoral psychotherapist Harvell Hendrix explains that a healthy marriage becomes a place to wrap up unfinished business from childhood. The healing process begins gradually by uncovering and acknowledging our unresolved childhood issues. The healing continues through the years as we allow our spouses to love us and as we learn how to love them.

Exploring Unfinished Business

Marriage is not a quick fix for avoiding your own personal problems. In fact, marriage may even intensify those problems. This exercise is designed to help you honestly face the psychological and spiritual work you need to do as a person so that you do not look to your spouse to fulfill needs that they simply cannot fulfill.

Everyone has yearnings that were seldom if ever fulfilled in their relationship with their parents. Take a moment to reflect, and then write down some of the needs and desires you felt were never really fulfilled for you by your parents. We've provided you with a few headings to stimulate your thinking, but don't let that limit your thinking to just these categories.

Unfulfilled Needs for Encouragement

Example: "My parents never really encouraged my dreams or goals."

_____

_____

_____

Unfulfilled Needs for Praise

Example: "My parents never really celebrated my successes."

_____

_____

_____

Unfulfilled Needs for Listening

Example: "My parents never really understood me for who I am."

_____

_____

_____

Unfulfilled Needs for Fun

Example: "My parents often thought I wasn't serious enough and wanted me to be more 'goal oriented.'"

_____

_____

_____

Other Unfulfilled Needs That Shape My Expectations

Example: "I've never had anyone in my life who appreciates my creativity."

_____

_____

_____

If you are willing, share your "unfinished business" with your partner and discuss the individual work each of you needs to do so that your marriage can be healthier and more harmonious.

 As you consider all the information you've covered in this guidebook, along with your sessions with your SYMBIS Facilitator, what are some of the most important lessons learned? How has this process changed your thinking, your feelings, your behavior for a better marriage?

TOGETHER FOREVER

As Good as It Gets is a comedy about an obsessive-compulsive author, Melvin Udall, played by Jack Nicholson.[3] Melvin Udall offends everyone he meets, but he becomes enamored with Carol Connelly, a struggling waitress played by Helen Hunt. She has seen Melvin at his worst but still agrees to meet him at a fancy restaurant for a date.

Carol arrives at the restaurant, feeling out of place and ill at ease as the staff waits on her hand and foot. The other patrons of the restaurant are impeccably dressed, while Carol wears a simple red dress, making her feel all the more insecure.

Melvin sees Carol and waves her over to his table. When she approaches, Melvin hits an all-time low. "This restaurant!" he says. "They make me buy a new outfit and let you in wearing a house dress." Carol is stunned and hurt by his incredulous insult but also knows it's part of the package with Melvin.

Carol looks him in the eye and says, "Pay me a compliment, Melvin. I need one now."

Melvin responds, "I've got a great compliment." What could he possibly say to undo the thoughtless comment he had just delivered?

Melvin then delivers one of the most romantic lines in big-screen history. This deeply flawed man with all his wounds, his own worst enemy, looks at Carol with all the kindness and sincerity his shriveled heart can muster and says, "Carol, you make me want to be a better man."

And she does. That's the payoff of a relationship made up of two wounded people. Glimmers of maturity shine through even in the midst of chaos—even in the midst of disharmony. That's the course of love between two imperfect people, mismatched like every other couple on the planet, but making each other want to be better. They do their best to find their footing, often losing their balance but then standing back up to keep moving forward.

Together.

NOTES

CHAPTER 3: WELLBEING

1. http://news.bbc.co.uk/2/hi/health/3105580.stm.
2. Ed Diener and Eunkook M. Suh, *Culture and Subjective Wellbeing* (Cambridge, MA: MIT Press, 2000).
3. B. Amsel, "The Separation/Individuation Process: The Struggle to Become an Adult." Retrieved from http://www.beverlyamselphd.com/separation-transition-to-adult (2009).

CHAPTER 4: SOCIAL LIFE

1. Jerry Seinfeld, *SeinLanguage* (New York: Bantam, 1995).
2. W. Bradford Wilcox and Nicholas Wolfinger, *Soul Mates: Religion, Sex, Love, and Marriage Among African Americans and Latinos*.
3. https://ifstudies.org/blog/faith-and-marriage-better-together.

CHAPTER 5: FINANCES

1. Michael J. Sandel, *What Money Can't Buy: The Moral Limits of Markets* (New York: Farrar, Straus and Giroux, reprint edition, 2013), 26, 138.
2. http://web.mit.edu/simester/Public/Papers/Alwaysleavehome.pdf.

CHAPTER 6: EXPECTATIONS

1. http://www.listsofnote.com/2012/04/einsteins-demands.html.

CHAPTER 7: REMARRIAGE AND BLENDING A FAMILY

1. There's a divorce rate measurement (age-standardized refined divorce rate) that provides an aggregate number. Many groups who study divorce use it, including the US Census Bureau. The best summary of divorce rates we know of is by Dr. Scott Stanley of the Institute for Family Studies, Jan. 22, 2015, http://slidingvsdeciding.blogspot.com/search?q =divorce+rate.

CHAPTER 10: LOVE LIFE

1. This is not a new phenomenon. A poll taken in 1966 reported that 76 percent of the married *couples* questioned named "love" as the major reason for marrying. Ten years later, in 1976, when a psychologist asked seventy-five thousand wives to evaluate the reasons for their decision to wed, she reported: "Love, love, love was far and away the front-runner." Paul Chance, "The Trouble with Love," *Psychology Today* (February 1988): 44–47.

2. http://content.nejm.org/cgi/content/extract/332/21/1452.

3. *20/20*, "Sex: Myths, Lies and Straight Talk," November 5, 2004.

4. A 1994 study by the National Opinion Research Center at the University of Chicago found that married couples in America generally enjoy more frequent and satisfying sexual activity than singles. Yet when married couples in America go to the movie theater or rent a video to catch Hollywood's latest hit, they're not likely to see couples on screen that are similar to them.

5. The survey was commissioned by the Family Research Council and data was collected from a nationwide random telephone sample of 1,100 people and conducted by an independent Bethesda firm and analyzed by an American University psychologist. Reported in *The Washington Post*, 1994, by William R Mattox, Jr. ("The Hottest Valentines").

6. R. T. Michael, J. H. Gagnon, and E. O. Lauman, *Sex in American: A Definitive Survey* (Boston: Little, Brown & Co., 1994), 124.

CHAPTER 11: ATTITUDE

1. Mary Landis and Judson Landis, *Building a Successful Marriage* (Englewood Cliffs, NJ: Prentice Hall, 1958).

2. I. Brissette, M. F. Scheier, and C. S. Carver, "The Role of Optimism and Social Network Development, Coping, and Psychological Adjustment During a Life Transition," *Journal of Personality and Social Psychology*, 82, 102–111 (2002). L. Kamen and M. E. P. Seligman, "Explanatory Style and Health." In M. Johnston and T. Marteau (eds.), "current psychological research and reviews:" Special issue on health psychology, 6, 207–218 (1987). L. Kamen and M. E. P. Seligman, explanatory style and health.

CHAPTER 12: COMMUNICATION

1. Valerian J. Derlega, "Developing Close Relationships," in Valerian J. Derlega, Sandra Metts, Sandra Petronio, and Stephen T. Margulis, *Self-Disclosure* (Newbury Park, CA: Sage, 1993).

2. Paul Tournier, *To Understand Each Other* (Atlanta: John Knox Press, 1967), 29.

CHAPTER 14: CONFLICT

1. "Fair Feud? 6 Issues Couples Should Argue About," MSNBC/Today, August 20, 2007, http://today.msnbc.msn.com/id/20323044.
2. Unhealthy conflict makes married couples more susceptible to illness and even prolongs the healing process of a wound.
3. K. T. Buehlman and John Gottman, "The Oral History Coding System," in *What Predicts Divorce? The Measures*, ed. John Gottman (Hillsdale, NJ: Erlbaum, 1996).
4. "Man Uses Air Raid Siren to Quiet Wife," CNN.com, April 19, 2003.

CHAPTER 15: SPIRITUALITY

1. Robert J. Sternberg, "Triangulating Love," in *The Altruism Reader: Selections from Writings on Love, Religion, and Science*, ed. Thomas Oord (West Conshohocken, PA: Templeton Press, 2007). Also Robert J. Sternberg, "A Triangular Theory of Love," in *Close Relationships*, ed. Harry T. Reis and Caryl E. Rusbult (New York: Psychology Press, 2004).
2. Daniel J. Hruschka, *Friendship: Development, Ecology, and Evolution of a Relationship* (Berkeley, CA: University of California Press, 2010).
3. Christopher R. Agnew et al., "Cognitive Interdependence: Commitment and the Mental Representation of Close Relationships," *Journal of Personality and Social Psychology* 74, no. 4 (1998): 939–54.
4. J. P Laurenceau et al., "Intimacy as an Interpersonal Process: Current Status and Future Directions," in *Handbook of Closeness and Intimacy*, ed. Debra J. Mashek and Arthur Aron (Mahwah, NJ: Erlbaum, 2004), 61–78.
5. K. J. Prager and L. J. Roberts, "Deep Intimate Connections: Self and Intimacy in Couple Relationships," in *Handbook of Closeness and Intimacy*, 43–60.
6. Daniel Akst, "America: Land of Loners?," *The Wilson Quarterly*, Summer 2010, http://www.wilsonquarterly.com/article.cfm?AID=1631.
7. Lisa A. Neff and Benjamin R. Karney, "The Dynamic Structure of Relationship Perceptions: Differential Importance as a Strategy of Relationship Maintenance," *Personality and Social Psychology Bulletin* 29, no. 11 (2003): 1433–46.
8. John Bowlby, *Loss: Sadness and Depression* vol. 3 of *Attachment and Loss*, ed. John Bowlby (New York: Basic Books, 1982).
9. Jeffrey Kluger, "The Biology of Belief," *Time*, February 12, 2009.
10. An increasing amount of scientific research is focusing on the relationship between religion and mental health. *Time* magazine reported some of the findings. Religious people are less depressed, less anxious, and less suicidal than nonreligious people, and they are better able to cope with such crises as illness and bereavement. Even if you compare two people who have symptoms of depression, says Michael McCullough, an associate professor of psychology and religious studies at the University of Miami, "the more religious person will be a little less sad."

11. Pamela Paul, "The Power of Uplift," *Time*, January 17, 2005.

12. Patricia Murphy of Rush University Medical Center in Chicago concluded a study she conducted on improved response to medical treatment by saying: "In our study, the positive response to medication had little to do with the feelings of hope that typically accompanies spiritual belief. It was tied specifically to the belief that a Supreme Being cared." February 23, 2010, http://www.rush.edu/webapps/MEDREL/servlet /NewsRelease?id=1353. The ultimate feeling of intimacy—that God *cares* for you— brings with it an inordinate amount of benefits, including a great deal of happiness.

13. Benjamin Vima, *Prayerfully Yours: Quality Prayer for Quality Life* (Bloomington, IN: Trafford Publishing, 2012).

14. Margaret M. Poloma and George H. Gallup, *Varieties of Prayer: A Survey Report* (Philadelphia: Trinity Press International, 1991).

15. C. S. Lewis, *Mere Christianity* (New York: Harper Collins, 1952), 50.

16. Forty-seven percent of people who report attending religious services several times a month describe themselves as "very happy," versus 28 percent of those who attend less than once a month. Kenneth I. Pargament and Annette Mahoney, "Spirituality: Discovering and Conserving the Sacred" in C. R. Snyder and Shane J. Lopez, eds., *Handbook of Positive Psychology*, 646–59.

17. According to the study, 70 percent of husbands who attend church regularly say they are "very happy" in their marriages, compared to only 59 percent of husbands who do not attend religious services. For women, the figures were similar, with a majority of those who attend church services reporting to be happier than those who do not. Read more at http://www.christianpost.com/news/church-attendance-key-to-marriage-success -researcher-says-33079/#rlpGtwPGUx1zbE81.99.

18. "Church Attendance Beneficial to Marriage, Researchers Says," CNSnews.com, July 7, 2008, http://www.cnsnews.com/news/article/church-attendance-beneficial-marriage -researcher-says.

19. D. A. Abbott, M. Berry, and W. H. Meredith, "Religious Belief and Practice: A Potential Asset in Helping Families," *Family Relations* (1990): 443–48.

CHAPTER 17: HARMONY

1. Joshua Wolf Shenk, "What Makes Us Happy?" *The Atlantic* (June 2009), 36–53.

2. J. F. Crosby, *Illusion and Disillusion: The Self in Love and Marriage*, 2nd ed. (Belmont, Calif.: Wadsworth, 1976). Also O. Kernberg, "Why Some People Can't Love," *Psychology Today* 12 (June 1978): 50–59.

3. *As Good as It Gets*, rated PG-13, a Columbia Tristar Picture (1997), directed by James L. Brooks, produced by Kristi Zea and Bridget Johnson, written by Mark Andrus and James L. Brooks

GIVE THE VERY BEST TO

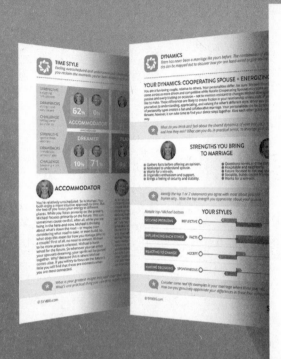

You won't find a more personalized and powerful pre-marriage assessment than SYMBIS.

"The SYMBIS Assessment rocks! We learned so much about our relationship and feel incredibly confident about our future together."
-Toni & Chris

Get your personalized 15-page report!

YOUR RELATIONSHIP

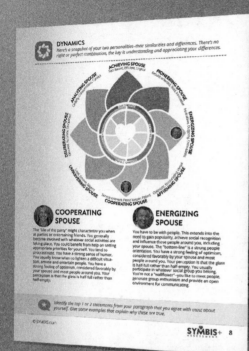

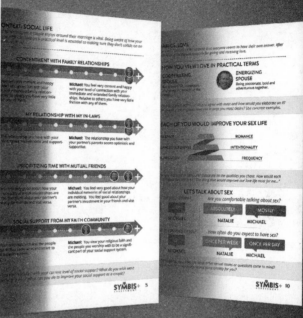

EVERYTHING YOU NEED TO KNOW ABOUT:

- **Your Personalities** – *discover your strengths*
- **Your Love Life** – *cultivate deeper passion*
- **Your Fight Types** – *discover your "hot topics"*
- **Your Talk Styles** – *crack your intimacy codes*
- **Your Money Methods** – *kick financial woes to the curb*

*And so much more. **Plus**, it works seamlessly with the SYMBIS book and his/her workbooks.*

*Take the assessment: **SYMBIS.com***

TAKE YOUR
NEXT STEPS

We've got everything you need and more:
LesandLeslie.com

COMMUNICATION

DRS. LES AND LESLIE PARROTT

Love Talk

SPEAK EACH OTHER'S LANGUAGE
LIKE YOU NEVER HAVE BEFORE

NEWLY UPDATED AND EXPANDED

SYMBIS+
ASSESSMENT

Report for:

NATALIE & MICHAEL BOERNER
Date Completed: 9/26/2017

Prepared by:
DRS. LES AND LESLIE PARROTT
info@LesandLeslie.com
206.123.4321

SYMBIS.com

THE
GOOD FIGHT

HOW CONFLICT CAN BRING YOU CLOSER

Drs. Les & Leslie Parrott
#1 NEW YORK TIMES BEST-SELLING AUTHORS

ASSESSMENT

CONFLICT